The art
and challenge
of translation

The art and challenge of translation

1 ST. PAUL
Philippians
Galatians

2 SAPPHO

3 J. F. KENNEDY IN LATIN

RAYMOND V. SCHODER, S.J.

BOLCHAZY-CARDUCCI PUBLISHERS
OAK PARK • ILLINOIS

COVER BY LEON DANILOVICS

Cover: St. Paul: 11 century mosaic at Hosios Loukas, Greece.
Photo: R. Schoder, SJ

PN
241
.A7
1987

This book was digitized via the Kurzweil scanner and typeset on Quadex 5000 and Compugraphic 8600 at Chicago Scan Typographers, Inc., a division of Bolchazy-Carducci Publishers, Inc.

© Copyright 1987
Bolchazy-Carducci Publishers, Inc.
44 Lake Street
Oak Park, Illinois 60302

Printed in the United States of America

International Standard Book Number
0-86516-182-8

Library of Congress Catalogue Number
86-72727

CONTENTS

Foreword	vi

PART 1

St. Paul

Philippians
Introduction	3
Text, Translation	8
Notes, Cross References	30

Galatians
Introduction	37
Text, Translation	40
Notes, Cross References	72

PART 2

Sappho
Introduction	87
Text and Translation	90

PART 3

J. F. Kennedy
Introduction	95
Text and Translation	98

Foreword

This publication is primarily intended as a teaching tool, a lesson in the problems and art of translation. It offers material in both prose and verse, into and out of English, to serve as examples for precise analysis by teacher and class and discussion of the diverse factors involved. The translations should be compared to their originals and appraised for accuracy and style, with consideration where they might be improved. This forces a close study of both texts, and calls on knowledge of grammar, vocabulary, and connotation in each language, thereby sharpening one's perception of intended meaning and idiomatic principles peculiar to the original language. It brings out a fuller, closer understanding of the inner principles, unique strengths, and limitations of the author's language and the level of skill with which it has been used in the piece being studied. It takes expression out of the abstract general plane of grammatical rules and vocabulary potential and brings it down to concrete usage in specifics. This promotes real grasp of the language in a way that mere reading often fails to achieve.

Translation is a delicate and complicated process. Its high goal is to present in another language (which has its own principles and rules) the precise message expressed by the author in his own tongue, as revealed by his choice of words and their effective, artistic sequence and collocation. It seeks to echo the original's true meaning in context, with its significant overtones, distinctive style, special individual use of words, and perceptible 'flavor'.

Translation must not slavishly copy a word-order or grammatical structure used by the author in apt observance of his own language's traditions, which may not be fully paralleled in the language of the translator. But the translated text must convey fully, according to the norms of its own language, the precise thought and personal style of the original. Mere literal transfer is not enough. The thought of the original must be carried over into the translation with exactness, neither altered nor diminished even if necessarily re-cast in order to observe the traditions and usage of the new language. The author's personal style has also to be mirrored faithfully, with its emotional qualities, distinctive manner, and artistic impact. The ultimate success would be to produce a piece in the new language that is so authentic in thought and expression in comparison with the original that readers might think the original author had written it himself in the new language as though it were his native tongue.

With the materials here provided from St. Paul, Sappho, and the Kennedy Inaugural, an alert teacher and group of advanced language students can investigate and evaluate how well these ideals of translation have been achieved, what in them is notably successful, what open to improvement in one way or another, the relative merits of alternative versions of the same material, and how they can themselves come up with a rendition more faithful or effective. Such exercise will bring a satisfying growth in comprehension of the original language and its distinctive subtleties when reading in it henceforth, and will be a fruitful and interesting form of composition. It will be an educative and humanistic experience, a demonstration of art as well as knowledge.

PART 1

St. PAUL
Philippians

Galatians

ΠΡΟΣ ΦΙΛΙΠΠΗΣΙΟΥΣ

Introduction

This beautiful epistle is rich in profound insights into the theology of Christ and is vibrant with Paul's apostolic love and concern. In it Paul reveals his human sensitivity and tenderness, his enthusiasm for Christ as the key to life, his closeness to his disciples, with whom he is willing to share not only his hopes and convictions but also his anxiety and fears and his ability to surmount both worry and affliction by a serene total confidence in God. Recurrent themes of this epistle are joy in the Lord and the urgent need of unity of faith based in true understanding of Christ and his unique role in mankind's salvation.

In Paul's day, Philippi was an important city in the Roman Province of Macedonia. Lying on the great Roman road from the Adriatic coast to Byzantium, the Via Egnatia, and in the midst of rich agricultural plains near the major gold resources of Mt. Pangaeus, it was essentially a Roman town, though with a large Greek/Macedonian population and a small contingent of Jews. Originally founded in the sixth century BC by nearby Thasos as Krenides, it was taken over in 356 BC by Philip II of Macedon, father of Alexander the Great, and re-named after him. Here in the adjacent plains, in October 42 BC, Antony and Octavian decisively defeated Brutus and Cassius, the slayers of Julius Caesar. Octavian later made Philippi a Roman colony and settled there many veterans of the Roman armies. Some 50 years later, Paul established at Philippi the first Christian community in Europe. His converts there remained especially close to him and dear to his heart, "my crown and joy" (4.1).

As recorded in *Acts* (16.9-39), Paul first came to Philippi, via its harbor Neapolis (modern Kavalla), on his second missionary journey, in 49 or 50 AD, accompanied by Timothy, Silas, and Luke. A prominent convert was the business woman Lydia, who gave them hospitality in her home. Paul exorcised a slave-girl whose clairvoyant spirit had been a source of income to her managers, and they stirred up the populace and magistrates to have Paul and Silas flogged as agitators and thrown into prison. When an earthquake that night freed them from their chains, their jailer released them and became a Christian, and Paul was officially escorted out of town, going to Thessalonike to the west, where his loyal Philippian converts continued to support him with financial help.

This letter to the faithful at Philippi was sent to them from prison elsewhere. It reports Paul's confinement for preaching Christ, the progress of the Gospel despite his afflictions, Paul's gratitude for their continuing concern and help, exhortations to growth in imitation of Christ and to joy in their faith and a holy unity of spirit, and warnings against the efforts of Judaizers among them to impose on them the burden of observing the Mosaic Law.

It is not certain where and when *Philippians* was written. Possibly during Paul's confinement at Rome from 61 to 63 AD (cp. *Acts* 28.14-31); perhaps when he was imprisoned at Caesarea in 58 (*Acts* 23.23—26.32); most likely at Ephesus around 56—seemingly referred to in 2 *Cor* 1.8: "we do not wish to leave you in the dark about the trouble we had in Asia; we were crushed beyond our strength, even to the point of despairing for life." (cp. also 1 *Cor* 15.32) Inscriptions prove that there was a Praitorion (Imperial Guard) at Ephesus, mentioned at 1.13, and it was much closer to Philippi than was Rome, making more feasible the several journeys back and forth referred to in the epistle. This would place the composition of *Philippians* within the period 54-58 AD when most of Paul's major epistles were written.

There is a likelihood that the epistle as we have it was put together from parts of three letters of Paul to his beloved

Philippians; or at least that it was composed at different periods, for there are notable variations in style and rather abrupt transitions from one section to another. Perhaps 1.1-2 + 4.10-20 is one letter of thanks for help, while 1.3—3.1 + 4.4-9 and 21-23 is another, with news of Paul's imprisonment and reports on Timothy and Epaphroditus, along with exhortations to the Philippians for Christian conduct, and 3.2—4.3 a third communication warning against the dangerous pressures from the Judaizers.

The symbol★ in the text means that there is an explanatory note on that word or passage at the end of each epistle. A raised small letter refers to other passages in Scripture with parallel or related content, as specified in the list of Cross References which follows the Notes.

The Greek text is reprinted from *The Greek New Testament*, edited by Aland, Black, Martini, Metzger, and Wickgren, third edition,* by permission of the publisher, United Bible Societies. The textual notes at the bottom of each page indicate manuscript variants. Explanatory notes to the content are provided, and references to parallel passages elsewhere in Scripture and identification of the location of Old Testament citations.

* (corrected)

PHILIPPI: VIA EGNATIA at foot of conical hill, with ruins of Forum on its left, Theater at right. (*Air Photo, R. Schoder, S.J.*)

ΠΡΟΣ ΦΙΛΙΠΠΗΣΙΟΥΣ

Salutation

1 Παῦλος καὶ Τιμόθεος δοῦλοι Χριστοῦ Ἰησοῦ πᾶσιν τοῖς ἁγίοις ἐν Χριστῷ Ἰησοῦ τοῖς οὖσιν ἐν Φιλίπποις σὺν ἐπισκόποις καὶ διακόνοις, 2 χάρις ὑμῖν καὶ εἰρήνη ἀπὸ θεοῦ πατρὸς ἡμῶν καὶ κυρίου Ἰησοῦ Χριστοῦ.

Paul's Prayer for the Philippians

3 Εὐχαριστῶ τῷ θεῷ μου ἐπὶ πάσῃ τῇ μνείᾳ ὑμῶν [a] 4 πάντοτε ἐν πάσῃ δεήσει μου ὑπὲρ πάντων ὑμῶν,[a] μετὰ χαρᾶς τὴν δέησιν ποιούμενος,[a] 5 ἐπὶ τῇ κοινωνίᾳ ὑμῶν εἰς τὸ εὐαγγέλιον ἀπὸ τῆς πρώτης ἡμέρας ἄχρι τοῦ νῦν, 6 πεποιθὼς αὐτὸ τοῦτο, ὅτι ὁ ἐναρξάμενος ἐν ὑμῖν ἔργον ἀγαθὸν ἐπιτελέσει ἄχρι ἡμέρας Χριστοῦ Ἰησοῦ· 7 καθώς ἐστιν δίκαιον ἐμοὶ τοῦτο φρονεῖν ὑπὲρ πάντων ὑμῶν διὰ τὸ ἔχειν με ἐν τῇ καρδίᾳ ὑμᾶς, ἔν τε τοῖς δεσμοῖς μου καὶ ἐν τῇ ἀπολογίᾳ καὶ βεβαιώσει τοῦ εὐαγγελίου συγκοινωνούς μου τῆς χάριτος πάντας ὑμᾶς ὄντας. 8 μάρτυς γάρ μου ὁ θεὸς ὡς ἐπιποθῶ πάντας ὑμᾶς ἐν σπλάγχνοις Χριστοῦ Ἰησοῦ. 9 καὶ τοῦτο προσεύχομαι,[b] ἵνα ἡ ἀγάπη ὑμῶν ἔτι μᾶλλον καὶ μᾶλλον περισσεύῃ ἐν ἐπιγνώσει καὶ πάσῃ αἰσθήσει 10 εἰς τὸ δοκιμάζειν ὑμᾶς τὰ διαφέροντα, ἵνα ἦτε εἰλικρινεῖς καὶ ἀπρόσκοποι εἰς ἡμέραν Χριστοῦ, 11 πεπληρωμένοι καρπὸν δικαιοσύνης τὸν διὰ Ἰησοῦ Χριστοῦ εἰς δόξαν καὶ ἔπαινον θεοῦ[1].

---

[1] 11 {B} καὶ ἔπαινον θεοῦ ℵ A B D^c I K P Ψ 33 81 88 104 181 326 330 436 451 614 629 630 1241 1739 1877 1881 1984 1985 2127 2492 2495 Byz Lect it^(c,d,dem,div,e,f,r1,x) vg syr^(p,h) cop^(sa,bo,fay) arm // καὶ ἔπαινον Χριστοῦ D^gr* 1962 // καὶ ἔπαινόν μοι F^gr G it^g Ambrosiaster // θεοῦ καὶ ἔπαινον ἐμοί p^16 (it^ar) // καὶ ἔπαινον αὐτοῦ it^z // καὶ ἔπαινον 1925

[a a a] 3-4 a none, a minor, a minor: WH // a minor, a none, a minor: TR Bov BF² AV RV ASV RSV (NEB) (Zür) (Jer) (Seg) // a dash, a none, a dash: Luth

[b] 9 b minor: TR Bov BF² AV RV ASV NEB Zür Luth Jer Seg // b none: WH RSV

---

2 Ro 1.7; Ga 1.3; Phm 3 3 Ro 1.8; 1 Cor 1.4 6 ὁ ἐναρξάμενος...ἀγαθόν Php 2.13 ἡμέρας Χριστοῦ Ἰησοῦ 1 Cor 1.8; Php 1.10; 2.16 8 μάρτυς...θεός Ro 1.9; 2 Cor 1.23; 1 Th 2.5 10 τὸ...διαφέροντα Ro 2.18; 12.2; He 5.14 ἡμέραν Χριστοῦ 1 Cor 1.8; Php 1.6; 2.16 11 Jn 15.8

■ CHAPTER ONE ■

Greeting

1 Paul and Timothy, slaves of Christ Jesus, to all in Philippi who have been sanctified* in Christ Jesus, and to their leaders and assistants*: 2 may you have favor and peace from God our father and from* the Lord Jesus Christ!a

I. INTRODUCTORY REFLECTIONS

Gratitude and Hope

3 I give thanks to my God every time I recall* you,b 4 always in all my prayers praying for all of you with joy, 5 because of the way you have continuously from the first day helped promote the Gospel and still do.

6 This I am sure of—that He who has begun in you a noble work will carry it through to completionc right up to the day of Christ Jesus.d 7 It is only natural that I should entertain such expectations in regard to all of you, since I hold all of you in my heart—you who are one and all sharers with me in God's favor, both in my imprisonment and in defense of the Gospel and its firm establishment. 8 God can testify in my supporte how much I long for each of you with the affection of Christ Jesus! 9 This is what I pray for: that your love may abound ever more and moref in perceptiveness and in every kind of awareness,* 10 so that you may learn to value those things that are really importantg and live in purity of conscience and blameless conduct right up to the day of Christ.h* 11 I pray that you may be rich in the harvest of that goodness which comes through Jesus Christ,i to the glory and praise of God.

To Me to Live is Christ

12 Γινώσκειν δὲ ὑμᾶς βούλομαι, ἀδελφοί, ὅτι τὰ κατ' ἐμὲ μᾶλλον εἰς προκοπὴν τοῦ εὐαγγελίου ἐλήλυθεν, 13 ὥστε τοὺς δεσμούς μου φανεροὺς ἐν Χριστῷ γενέσθαι ἐν ὅλῳ τῷ πραιτωρίῳ καὶ τοῖς λοιποῖς πᾶσιν, 14 καὶ τοὺς πλείονας τῶν ἀδελφῶν ἐν κυρίῳ πεποιθότας τοῖς δεσμοῖς μου περισσοτέρως τολμᾶν ἀφόβως τὸν λόγον λαλεῖν[2].

15 Τινὲς μὲν καὶ διὰ φθόνον καὶ ἔριν, τινὲς δὲ καὶ δι' εὐδοκίαν τὸν Χριστὸν κηρύσσουσιν· 16[c] οἱ μὲν ἐξ ἀγάπης, εἰδότες ὅτι εἰς ἀπολογίαν τοῦ εὐαγγελίου κεῖμαι, 17[c] οἱ δὲ ἐξ ἐριθείας τὸν Χριστὸν καταγγέλλουσιν, οὐχ ἁγνῶς, οἰόμενοι θλῖψιν ἐγείρειν τοῖς δεσμοῖς μου. 18 τί γάρ; πλὴν ὅτι παντὶ τρόπῳ, εἴτε προφάσει εἴτε ἀληθείᾳ, Χριστὸς καταγγέλλεται, καὶ ἐν τούτῳ χαίρω. ἀλλὰ καὶ χαρήσομαι, 19 οἶδα γὰρ ὅτι τοῦτό μοι ἀποβήσεται εἰς σωτηρίαν διὰ τῆς ὑμῶν δεήσεως καὶ ἐπιχορηγίας τοῦ πνεύματος Ἰησοῦ Χριστοῦ 20 κατὰ τὴν ἀποκαραδοκίαν καὶ ἐλπίδα μου, ὅτι ἐν οὐδενὶ αἰσχυνθήσομαι ἀλλ' ἐν πάσῃ παρρησίᾳ ὡς πάντοτε καὶ νῦν μεγαλυνθήσεται Χριστὸς ἐν τῷ σώματί μου, εἴτε διὰ ζωῆς εἴτε διὰ θανάτου. 21 ἐμοὶ γὰρ τὸ ζῆν Χριστὸς καὶ τὸ ἀποθανεῖν

---

[2] 14 {D} λόγον λαλεῖν 𝔓[46] D[c] K 181 614 630 1739 1881 (1984 transposes: λαλεῖν τὸν λόγον) (1985 transposes: λαλῶν τὸν λόγον) (2495 λόγον λαβεῖν) Byz Lect it[rl] syr[h] Marcion Chrysostom Theodoret John-Damascus ∥ λόγον κυρίου λαλεῖν G it[g] Cyprian ∥ λόγον τοῦ θεοῦ λαλεῖν ℵ A B P Ψ 33 81 88 104 326 330 436 451 629 1241 1877 1962 2127 2492 it[ar,c,dem,div,f,x,z] vg syr[p,h] with * cop[sa,bo,fay] goth arm eth Clement Ambrosiaster[txt] Chrysostom Euthalius ∥ λόγον λαλεῖν τοῦ θεοῦ D* it[d,e] Ambrosiaster[comm] ∥ τοῦ θεοῦ λόγον λαλεῖν 42 234 483

[c c] 16-17 c verse 16, c verse 17: WH Bov BF² RV ASV RSV NEB Zür Luth Jer Seg ∥ c verse 17 (numbered 16), c verse 16 (numbered 17): TR AV

---

12 τὰ...ἐλήλυθεν 2 Tm 2.9   13 τοὺς δεσμούς μου Eph 3.1; 4.1; Phm 1, 9   19 τοῦτο... σωτηρίαν Job 13.16   διὰ...δεήσεως 2 Cor 1.11   20 ἐν οὐδενὶ...Χριστός 1 Pe 4.16   21 ἐμοὶ ...Χριστός Ga 2.20

Progress of the Gospel

12 My brethren,* I want you to know that what has happened to me has actually turned out to the further advance of the Gospel. 13 The result has been that my imprisonment has become well known throughout the official Guard here and to all the others also as being in the cause of Christ,[a] 14 and the majority of my fellow believers in the Lord, taking courage from my very chains, have been emboldened even more than before to proclaim the Message fearlessly. 15 True, some preach Christ from motives that involve envy and rivalry, others from friendly good intentions. 16 These act from kindly love, aware that I am confined here for the defense of the Gospel; 17 the others promote Christ not from pure motives but selfishly, as an intrigue against me, thinking that it will make my imprisonment more harsh. 18 What of it? All that matters is that in any and every way, whether hypocritically or sincerely, Christ is being proclaimed! And that brings me joy. Indeed I will continue happy 19 in the conviction that this will turn out to my salvation,[b]* thanks to your prayers[c] and to the support I will receive from the Spirit of Jesus Christ. 20 I vividly expect and trust that I will never be disgraced by failure, but that with all courage now as always Christ will be glorified in my body,[d] whether I live or die.*

21 For to me, living means Christ,[e]* and to die would be

κέρδος. 22 εἰ δὲ τὸ ζῆν ἐν σαρκί,^d τοῦτό μοι καρπὸς ἔργου,^d καὶ τί αἱρήσομαι^e οὐ γνωρίζω. 23 συνέχομαι δὲ ἐκ τῶν δύο, τὴν ἐπιθυμίαν ἔχων εἰς τὸ ἀναλῦσαι καὶ σὺν Χριστῷ εἶναι, πολλῷ [γὰρ] μᾶλλον κρεῖσσον· 24 τὸ δὲ ἐπιμένειν [ἐν] τῇ σαρκὶ ἀναγκαιότερον δι' ὑμᾶς. 25 καὶ τοῦτο πεποιθὼς^f οἶδα^f ὅτι μενῶ καὶ παραμενῶ πᾶσιν ὑμῖν εἰς τὴν ὑμῶν προκοπὴν καὶ χαρὰν τῆς πίστεως, 26 ἵνα τὸ καύχημα ὑμῶν περισσεύῃ ἐν Χριστῷ Ἰησοῦ ἐν ἐμοὶ διὰ τῆς ἐμῆς παρουσίας πάλιν πρὸς ὑμᾶς.

27 Μόνον ἀξίως τοῦ εὐαγγελίου τοῦ Χριστοῦ πολιτεύεσθε, ἵνα εἴτε ἐλθὼν καὶ ἰδὼν ὑμᾶς εἴτε ἀπὼν ἀκούω τὰ περὶ ὑμῶν, ὅτι στήκετε ἐν ἑνὶ πνεύματι, μιᾷ ψυχῇ συναθλοῦντες τῇ πίστει τοῦ εὐαγγελίου 28 καὶ μὴ πτυρόμενοι ἐν μηδενὶ ὑπὸ τῶν ἀντικειμένων, ^gἥτις ἐστὶν αὐτοῖς ἔνδειξις ἀπωλείας, ὑμῶν δὲ σωτηρίας, καὶ τοῦτο ἀπὸ θεοῦ· 29 ὅτι ὑμῖν ἐχαρίσθη τὸ ὑπὲρ Χριστοῦ, οὐ μόνον τὸ εἰς αὐτὸν πιστεύειν ἀλλὰ καὶ τὸ ὑπὲρ αὐτοῦ πάσχειν,^g 30 τὸν αὐτὸν ἀγῶνα ἔχοντες, οἷον εἴδετε ἐν ἐμοὶ καὶ νῦν ἀκούετε ἐν ἐμοί.

Christian Humility and Christ's Humility

2 Εἴ τις οὖν παράκλησις ἐν Χριστῷ, εἴ τι παραμύθιον ἀγάπης, εἴ τις κοινωνία πνεύματος, εἴ τις σπλάγχνα καὶ οἰκτιρμοί, 2 πληρώσατέ μου τὴν χαρὰν ἵνα τὸ αὐτὸ φρονῆτε, τὴν αὐτὴν ἀγάπην ἔχοντες, σύμψυχοι, τὸ ἕν¹

---

¹ 2 {B} ἕν p⁴⁶ N^c B D G K P 88 104 181 326 330 436 451 614 629 630 1739

^d ^d 22 d minor, d minor: WH^mg BF² // d minor, d major: TR Bov AV RV^mg ASV^mg RSV // d none, d minor: Zür (Luth) Jer // d dash, d minor: RV ASV // d minor, d dash: WH // d none, d question: NEB Seg

^e 22 e none: TR WH Bov BF² AV RV ASV RSV (Zür) (Luth) Jer // e question: WH^mg RV^mg ASV^mg NEB Seg

^f ^f 25 f none, f none: WH // f none, f minor: TR Bov BF² NEB (Seg) // f minor, f none: AV RV ASV RSV (Zür) (Luth) Jer

^g ^g 28-29 g g no parens: TR Bov BF² AV RV ASV RSV NEB Zür Luth Jer Seg // g parens, g parens: WH

22 τοῦτο...ἔργου Ro 1.13   23 τὴν ἐπιθυμίαν...κρεῖσσον 2 Cor 5.8   27 Μόνον... πολιτεύεσθε Eph 4.1; Col 1.10; 1 Th 2.12   συναθλοῦντες...εὐαγγελίου Php 4.3   30 τὸν... εἴδετε ἐν ἐμοί Ac 16.22   νῦν...ἐμοί Php 1.13

profit. 22 If however I am to go on living in the flesh, that means fruitful labor for me[a]—and I do not know which to prefer. 23 I am strongly attracted by both possibilities: I long to depart this life and be with Christ[b]; [for] that is by far the best. 24 Yet it is more urgent that I remain in the flesh, for your sakes. 25 And I know without doubt that I will remain and continue with you all, to the advantage of your progress and joy in the faith, 26 so that because of my being with you again* you may have in me abundant cause to exult in Christ.

II. PLEAS FOR CHRISTIAN HEROISM

Courage in Professing the Faith

27 Anyhow, conduct yourselves worthily of the good news of Christ,[c] so that whether I come and see you myself or hear about your behavior from afar, I will find that you are standing firm in unity of spirit, with a single heart exerting yourselves in unison that the Gospel my be believed.[d] 28 Do not be intimidated in any situation by your opponents! Their opposition is a foreshadowing of their own destruction—but of your salvation. All this is God's doing—29 for it is your special privilege to take Christ's side—not only to believe in him but to suffer for him also.[e] 30 Yours is the very same struggle as mine, such as you saw me undergo and now hear that I am in.[f]

■ CHAPTER TWO ■

Imitate Christ's Humility

1 Therefore, in the name of the consolation and encouragement that you owe me in Christ, of the solace that love can give, of fellowship in spirit, of compassion and pity, I beg you: 2 bring my joy to the full by being of one mind, with one and the same love, united in spirit and in ideals.[g]

φρονοῦντες, 3 μηδὲν κατ' ἐριθείαν μηδὲ κατὰ κενοδοξίαν ἀλλὰ τῇ ταπεινοφροσύνῃ ἀλλήλους ἡγούμενοι ὑπερέχοντας ἑαυτῶν, 4 μὴ τὰ ἑαυτῶν ἕκαστος σκοποῦντες ἀλλὰ [καὶ] τὰ ἑτέρων[a] ἕκαστοι[2].[a] 5 τοῦτο[3] φρονεῖτε ἐν ὑμῖν ὃ καὶ ἐν Χριστῷ Ἰησοῦ, 6 ὃς ἐν μορφῇ θεοῦ ὑπάρχων οὐχ ἁρπαγμὸν ἡγήσατο τὸ εἶναι ἴσα θεῷ, 7 ἀλλὰ ἑαυτὸν ἐκένωσεν μορφὴν δούλου λαβών, ἐν ὁμοιώματι ἀνθρώπων γενόμενος· [b]καὶ σχήματι εὑρεθεὶς ὡς ἄνθρωπος 8[b] ἐταπείνωσεν ἑαυτὸν γενόμενος ὑπήκοος μέχρι θανάτου, θανάτου δὲ σταυροῦ. 9 διὸ καὶ ὁ θεὸς αὐτὸν ὑπερύψωσεν καὶ ἐχαρίσατο αὐτῷ τὸ ὄνομα τὸ ὑπὲρ πᾶν ὄνομα, 10 ἵνα ἐν τῷ ὀνόματι Ἰησοῦ πᾶν γόνυ κάμψῃ ἐπουρανίων καὶ ἐπιγείων καὶ καταχθονίων 11 καὶ πᾶσα γλῶσσα ἐξομολογήσηται ὅτι κύριος Ἰησοῦς Χριστὸς εἰς δόξαν θεοῦ πατρός.

1877 1881 1984 1985 2127 2492 2495 *Byz Lect* it[d,e,g,m] syr[p,h] arm? eth Clement Ambrosiaster Victorinus-Rome Hilary Basil Pelagius Augustine ∥ αὐτό ℵ* A C I Ψ 33 81 1241 1962 it[ar,c,dem,div,f,x,z] vg goth Euthalius
[2] 4 {B} ἕκαστοι p[46] ℵ A B D[gr] P Ψ 33 81 104 1241 1739 1881 1962 2127 Victorinus-Rome Basil Augustine Cyril Euthalius ∥ ἕκαστος K 88 181 326 330 436 451 614 629 630 1877 1984 1985 2492 2495 *Byz Lect* it[d,e] syr[p,h] (cop[bo?]) goth arm Chrysostom Jerome Theodoret John-Damascus ∥ *omit* G it[ar,c,dem,div,f,g,m,x,z] vg cop[sa] eth Ambrosiaster Pelagius
[3] 5 {C} τοῦτο ℵ* A B C Ψ 33 81 1241 1985 2495 (*Lect beginning of lection*) it[t] cop[sa,bo] arm eth Origen Augustine Euthalius ∥ τοῦτο γάρ p[46] ℵ[c] D G K P 88 104 181 326 436 614 629 630 1739 1877 1881 1962 1984 2127 *Byz* it[ar,c,d,dem,div,e,f,g,m,x,z] vg syr[h,pal] goth Ambrosiaster Victorinus-Rome Hilary Chrysostom Theodoret John-Damascus ∥ τοῦτο οὖν 330 451 2492 ∥ καὶ τοῦτο syr[p]

[a a] **4-5** *a* none, *a* major: WH Bov BF² AV? RV ASV RSV NEB Zür Jer Seg ∥ *a* major, *a* none: WH[mg] Luth ∥ different text: TR AV?

[b b] **7-8** *b* no number, *b* number 8: TR[ed] WH Bov BF² Zür Luth Jer ∥ *b* number 8, *b* no number: TR[ed] AV RV ASV RSV NEB Seg

---

3 μηδὲ κατὰ κενοδοξίαν Ga 5.26 ἀλλήλους...ἑαυτῶν Ro 12.10   **4** 1 Cor 10.24, 33
6 οὐχ...θεῷ Jn 1.1, 2; 17.5   **7** ἑαυτὸν ἐκένωσεν 2 Cor 8.9   ἐν...γενόμενος Jn 1.14; Ro 8.3;
He 2.14, 17   **8** ἐταπείνωσεν...θανάτου Jn 10.17; He 5.8; 12.2   **9** ὁ θεὸς αὐτὸν ὑπερύψωσεν
Ac 2.33; He 1.3 ἐχαρίσατο...ὄνομα Eph 1.21; He 1.4   **10-11** πᾶν...ἐξομολογήσηται Is 45.23;
Ro 14.11

3 Never act out of selfish rivalry or shallow conceit[a]; rather, think of one another in humility as superior to yourselves,[b] each of you looking to others' interests rather than his own.[c]

5 Your attitude must be the same as Christ's:★

>6 Being in fact divine,[d]
>he did not consider it usurpation★
>to be equal to God.
>7 Nevertheless he dispossessed himself,[e]★
>taking the condition of a slave★
>by being known as a man, human in form,[f]★
>8 he humbled himself,
>making himself obedient even to accepting death,[g]
>yes, death on a cross!★
>9 Because of this,
>God in turn exalted him on high[h]
>and bestowed on him the privilege of the name
>which is above every other name,[i]★
>10 whose dignity requires
>that at the mention of Jesus' name
>every knee must bend[j]★
>of all beings that exist
>in the heavens and on earth and under the earth,
>11 and every tongue proclaim
>JESUS CHRIST IS LORD![k]
>to the glory of God the father.

Shining as Lights in the World

12 Ὥστε, ἀγαπητοί μου, καθὼς πάντοτε ὑπηκούσατε, μὴ ὡς⁴ ἐν τῇ παρουσίᾳ μου μόνον ἀλλὰ νῦν πολλῷ μᾶλλον ἐν τῇ ἀπουσίᾳ μου, μετὰ φόβου καὶ τρόμου τὴν ἑαυτῶν σωτηρίαν κατεργάζεσθε· 13 θεὸς γάρ ἐστιν ὁ ἐνεργῶν ἐν ὑμῖν καὶ τὸ θέλειν καὶ τὸ ἐνεργεῖν ὑπὲρ τῆς εὐδοκίας. 14 πάντα ποιεῖτε χωρὶς γογγυσμῶν καὶ διαλογισμῶν, 15 ἵνα γένησθε ἄμεμπτοι καὶ ἀκέραιοι, τέκνα θεοῦ ἄμωμα μέσον γενεᾶς σκολιᾶς καὶ διεστραμμένης,ᶜ ἐν οἷς φαίνεσθε ὡς φωστῆρες ἐν κόσμῳ, 16 λόγον ζωῆς ἐπέχοντες, εἰς καύχημα ἐμοὶ εἰς ἡμέραν Χριστοῦ, ὅτι οὐκ εἰς κενὸν ἔδραμον οὐδὲ εἰς κενὸν ἐκοπίασα. 17 ἀλλὰ εἰ καὶ σπένδομαι ἐπὶ τῇ θυσίᾳ καὶ λειτουργίᾳ τῆς πίστεως ὑμῶν, χαίρω καὶ συγχαίρω πᾶσιν ὑμῖν· 18 τὸ δὲ αὐτὸ καὶ ὑμεῖς χαίρετε καὶ συγχαίρετέ μοι.

Timothy and Epaphroditus

19 Ἐλπίζω δὲ ἐν κυρίῳ Ἰησοῦ Τιμόθεον ταχέως πέμψαι ὑμῖν, ἵνα κἀγὼ εὐψυχῶ γνοὺς τὰ περὶ ὑμῶν. 20 οὐδένα γὰρ ἔχω ἰσόψυχον, ὅστις γνησίως τὰ περὶ ὑμῶν μεριμνήσει· 21 οἱ πάντες γὰρ τὰ ἑαυτῶν ζητοῦσιν, οὐ τὰ Ἰησοῦ Χριστοῦ. 22 τὴν δὲ δοκιμὴν αὐτοῦ γινώσκετε, ὅτι ὡς πατρὶ τέκνον σὺν ἐμοὶ ἐδούλευσεν εἰς τὸ εὐαγγέλιον.

---

⁴ 12 {B} ὡς p⁴⁶ ℵ A C D G K P Ψ 81 88 104 181 326 330 436 451 614 629 630 1739 1877 1881 1962 1984 1985 2127 2492 2495 *Byz Lect* itᵃʳ,ᶜ,ᵈ,ᵈᵉᵐ,ᵈⁱᵛ*,ᵉ,f,g,x,z* vg syrʰ *∥ omit* B 33 42 234 618 1241 itᵈⁱᵛᶜ,ᶻᶜ syrᵖ copˢᵃ,ᵇᵒ arm eth Ambrosiaster Chrysostom Cassiodorus

---

ᶜ 15 *c* minor: TR WH Bov BF² AV RV ASV RSV NEB Zür Luth Jer Seg ∥ *c* major: NEBᵐᵍ

---

12 μετὰ...κατεργάζεσθε Ps 2.11; 1 Pe 1.17   13 θεὸς...ὑμῖν Jn 15.5; 1 Cor 12.6; 15.10; 2 Cor 3.5; 1 Th 2.13   14 πάντα...γογγυσμῶν 1 Cor 10.10; 1 Pe 4.9   15 γενεᾶς...διεστραμμένης Dt 32.5; Mt 10.16; Ac 2.40   ἐν...κόσμῳ Dn 12.3; Mt 5.14; Eph 5.8   16 λόγον...ἐμοί 1 Th 2.19   ἡμέραν Χριστοῦ 1 Cor 1.8; Php 1.6, 10   οὐκ...ἐκοπίασα Is 49.4; 65.23; Ga 2.2   17 σπένδομαι...ὑμῶν Ro 15.16; 2 Tm 4.6   18 τὸ...χαίρετε Php 3.1; 4.4   21 2 Tm 4.10

The Innocence of Children of God

12 So then, my dearly beloved, obedient as always to my urging, work with anxious concern* to achieve your salvation,[a] not only as when I am with you but all the more now when I am absent. **13** For it is God who in his kindly concern for you produces in you both the desire and its carrying out.[b] **14** In everything you do, act without grumbling or arguing[c]; **15** seek to be blameless and single-minded, children of God beyond reproach in the midst of a generation that is twisted and depraved[d]—among whom you shine forth like sources of light in the world[e] **16** as you hold toward it* the Word of Life. Thus for the day of Christ you give me cause to boast[f] that I did not run the race in vain nor toil without result.[g] **17** Yes, even if I am poured out as a libation[h]* over the sacrificial ceremony of your faith, I am glad of it and rejoice with all of you. **18** Do you also be glad[i] on the same score, and rejoice along with me!

III. NEWS OF PAUL'S ASSISTANTS AND PLANS

Timothy

19 I hope, too, in the Lord Jesus, to send Timothy[j] to you soon, that I too may be consoled—by learning the news about you. **20** For I have no one comparable to him for genuine interest in whatever concerns you. **21** Everyone, alas, seeks his own interests[k] rather than those of Jesus Christ. **22** You know from experience his quality, how he was like a son at his father's side serving along with me the cause of the Gospel.

23 τοῦτον μὲν οὖν ἐλπίζω πέμψαι ὡς ἂν ἀφίδω τὰ περὶ ἐμὲ ἐξαυτῆς· 24 πέποιθα δὲ ἐν κυρίῳ ὅτι καὶ αὐτὸς ταχέως ἐλεύσομαι.

25 Ἀναγκαῖον δὲ ἡγησάμην Ἐπαφρόδιτον τὸν ἀδελφὸν καὶ συνεργὸν καὶ συστρατιώτην μου, ὑμῶν δὲ ἀπόστολον καὶ λειτουργὸν τῆς χρείας μου, πέμψαι πρὸς ὑμᾶς, 26 ἐπειδὴ ἐπιποθῶν ἦν πάντας ὑμᾶς[5] καὶ ἀδημονῶν, διότι ἠκούσατε ὅτι ἠσθένησεν. 27 καὶ γὰρ ἠσθένησεν παραπλήσιον θανάτῳ· ἀλλὰ ὁ θεὸς ἠλέησεν αὐτόν, οὐκ αὐτὸν δὲ μόνον ἀλλὰ καὶ ἐμέ, ἵνα μὴ λύπην ἐπὶ λύπην σχῶ. 28 σπουδαιοτέρως οὖν ἔπεμψα αὐτόν, ἵνα ἰδόντες αὐτὸν πάλιν χαρῆτε κἀγὼ ἀλυπότερος ὦ. 29 προσδέχεσθε οὖν αὐτὸν ἐν κυρίῳ μετὰ πάσης χαρᾶς καὶ τοὺς τοιούτους ἐντίμους ἔχετε, 30 ὅτι διὰ τὸ ἔργον Χριστοῦ[6] μέχρι θανάτου ἤγγισεν παραβολευσάμενος τῇ ψυχῇ, ἵνα ἀναπληρώσῃ τὸ ὑμῶν ὑστέρημα τῆς πρός με λειτουργίας.

The True Righteousness

3 Τὸ λοιπόν, ἀδελφοί μου, χαίρετε ἐν κυρίῳ. τὰ αὐτὰ γράφειν ὑμῖν ἐμοὶ μὲν οὐκ ὀκνηρόν, ὑμῖν δὲ ἀσφαλές.

---

[5] **26** {C} ὑμᾶς ℵ^c (B transposes: ὑμᾶς πάντας) G K P Ψ 181 614 629 630 1739 1881 *Byz Lect* it^(ar,c,dem,div,f,g,x,z) vg cop^sa goth (Ambrosiaster) Victorinus-Rome Chrysostom Theodoret Cassiodorus^(1/2) ‖ ὑμᾶς ἰδεῖν ℵ* A C D I^vid 33 81 88 104 326 330 436 451 1241 1877 1962 1984 1985 2127 2492 2495 it^(d,e) syr^(p,h,pal) cop^bo arm eth Euthalius Cassiodorus^(1/2) John-Damascus Theophylact ‖ πρὸς ὑμᾶς *(after gap)* p^46

[6] **30** {C} Χριστοῦ p^46 B G 88 436 1739 1881 Origen ‖ τοῦ Χριστοῦ D K 181 326 614 629 630 1877 1984 2495 *Byz Lect* Chrysostom^txt Theodoret John-Damascus ‖ Χριστοῦ *or* τοῦ Χριστοῦ it^(ar,c,d,dem,div,e,f,g,x,z) vg syr^p cop^sa goth Ambrosiaster Victorinus-Rome ‖ κυρίου ℵ A P Ψ 33 81 104 330 451 1241 1962 2127 2492 syr^h cop^bo arm eth Euthalius ‖ τοῦ θεοῦ 1985 Chrysostom ‖ *omit* C

---

25 ὑμῶν δὲ...χρείας μου Php 4.18   29 1 Cor 16.16, 18; 1 Tm 5.17
3 1 χαίρετε ἐν κυρίῳ Php 2.18; 4.4

23 It is he, then, whom I hope to send as soon as I see how things are going with me. 24 In fact, I am confident in the Lord that I myself will also come soon.*

Epaphroditus

25 I have decided too that I must send you Epaphroditus,[a] my brother and co-worker and fellow-soldier, whom you sent to take care of my needs. 26 He has been longing for all of you and was distressed that you heard about his sickness—27 for he was ill to the verge of death. But God pitied him; rather, not just him but also me, to save me from sorrow heaped on sorrow. 28 It is with a special urgency, therefore, that I have sent him, so that you may renew your joy on seeing him, and my own anxieties may be lessened thereby. 29 Welcome him then in the Lord with full joy, and hold such men in esteem,[b] 30 for he came near to death for the sake of Christ's work, risking his life in an effort to make up for those services to me which you could not perform.

IV. CHRISTIAN DEDICATION

■ CHAPTER THREE ■

Breaking with Judaism

1 For the rest, my brethren, rejoice* in the Lord.[c] Writing the same things to you is not a burden for me and is for you a safeguard.

2 Βλέπετε τοὺς κύνας, βλέπετε τοὺς κακοὺς ἐργάτας, βλέπετε τὴν κατατομήν. 3 ἡμεῖς γάρ ἐσμεν ἡ περιτομή, οἱ πνεύματι θεοῦ¹ λατρεύοντες καὶ καυχώμενοι ἐν Χριστῷ Ἰησοῦ καὶ οὐκ ἐν σαρκὶ πεποιθότες, 4 καίπερ ἐγὼ ἔχων πεποίθησιν καὶ ἐν σαρκί. εἴ τις δοκεῖ ἄλλος πεποιθέναι ἐν σαρκί, ἐγὼ μᾶλλον· 5 περιτομῇ ὀκταήμερος, ἐκ γένους Ἰσραήλ, φυλῆς Βενιαμίν, Ἑβραῖος ἐξ Ἑβραίων, κατὰ νόμον Φαρισαῖος, 6 κατὰ ζῆλος διώκων τὴν ἐκκλησίαν, κατὰ δικαιοσύνην τὴν ἐν νόμῳ γενόμενος ἄμεμπτος. 7 [ἀλλὰ] ἅτινα ἦν μοι κέρδη, ταῦτα ἥγημαι διὰ τὸν Χριστὸν ζημίαν. 8 ἀλλὰ μενοῦνγε καὶ ἡγοῦμαι πάντα ζημίαν εἶναι διὰ τὸ ὑπερέχον τῆς γνώσεως Χριστοῦ Ἰησοῦ τοῦ κυρίου μου, δι' ὃν τὰ πάντα ἐζημιώθην, καὶ ἡγοῦμαι σκύβαλα, ἵνα Χριστὸν κερδήσω 9 καὶ εὑρεθῶ ἐν αὐτῷ, μὴ ἔχων ἐμὴν δικαιοσύνην τὴν ἐκ νόμου ἀλλὰ τὴν διὰ πίστεως Χριστοῦ, τὴν ἐκ θεοῦ δικαιοσύνην ἐπὶ τῇ πίστει, 10 τοῦ γνῶναι αὐτὸν καὶ τὴν δύναμιν τῆς ἀναστάσεως αὐτοῦ καὶ [τὴν] κοινωνίαν [τῶν] παθημάτων αὐτοῦ, συμμορφιζόμενος τῷ θανάτῳ αὐτοῦ, 11 εἴ πως καταντήσω εἰς τὴν ἐξανάστασιν τὴν ἐκ νεκρῶν.

---

¹ 3 {C} θεοῦ ℵ* A B C Dᶜ G K 33 81 104 181 326 330 451 614 629 630 1241 1739 1877 1881 1985 2492 2495 *Byz Lect* itᵍ syrʰᵐᵍ cop^(sa,bo) arm? Origen Eusebius Athanasius Greek mss^(acc. to Ambrose) Ambrose Didymus^(lat) Greek and Latin mss^(acc. to Augustine) Augustine Euthalius Theodoret John-Damascus ∥ θεῷ ℵᶜ D* P Ψ 88 436 1962 (1984 θείῳ) 2127 it^(ar,c,d,dem,div,e,f,m,x,z) vg syr^(p,h) goth arm? eth Origen^(gr,lat) Ambrosiaster Victorinus-Rome Latin mss^(acc. to Ambrose) Chrysostom Theodore^(lat) Greek and Latin mss^(acc. to Augustine) Theodoret ∥ omit p¹⁶

---

2 Βλέπετε τοὺς κύνας Ps 22.16, 20; Re 22.15 3 Ro 2.29 4 ἐγὼ ἔχων...σαρκί 2 Cor 11.18 5 περιτομῇ ὀκταήμερος Lk 1.59; 2.21 ἐκ...Ἑβραίων 2 Cor 11.22 κατὰ νόμον Φαρισαῖος Ac 23.6; 26.5 6 διώκων τὴν ἐκκλησίαν Ac 8.3; 22.4; 26.9-11 7 Mt 13.44, 46; Lk 14.33 9 τὴν διὰ...πίστει Ro 3.21-22 10 τὴν...αὐτοῦ, συμμορφιζόμενος...αὐτοῦ Ro 6.3-5 τὴν κοινωνίαν τῶν παθημάτων αὐτοῦ Ro 8.17; Ga 6.17 11 καταντήσω...νεκρῶν Ac 4.2; Re 20.5-6

2 Beware of the dogs!ᵃ Beware of the evil-doers! Beware of the practice of mutilation!★ **3** It is we in fact who are the Circumcision,ᵇ★ we who worship by the Spirit of God,★ who glory in Christ Jesus and do not put our reliance in flesh— **4** though I myself can be confident even there. If anyone else thinks he has a right to put his trust in flesh, all the more can I!ᶜ **5** I was circumcised on the eighth day,ᵈ★ being of the race of Israel and the tribe of Benjamin, a Hebrew of Hebrew parentage,ᵉ in legal observance a Pharisee,ᶠ★ **6** so zealous that I persecuted the Church;ᵍ I was above reproach in regard to that justice which is based on the Law.

7 [But] now those very things that I used to think assets I have come to consider in the light of Christ as a liability.ʰ★ **8** In fact, I actually rate all as loss because of the supreme good of knowing Jesus Christ my Lord. For his sake I have accepted total loss of all things and I value them as mere dung, so that Christ may be my wealth **9** and I may be found in him, not holding to any justice of my own based on observance of the Law, but possessing that justice which comes through faith in Christ★—the justice which comes from God and is based on faith.ⁱ **10** I wish thus to know Christ and the power flowing from his resurrection and how to share in his sufferings by being formed into the pattern of his death,ʲ **11** in the hope that thus I may arrive at the resurrection from the dead.ᵏ

Pressing toward the Mark

12 Οὐχ ὅτι ἤδη ἔλαβον ἢ ἤδη τετελείωμαι², διώκω δὲ εἰ καὶ καταλάβω, ἐφ' ᾧ καὶ κατελήμφθην ὑπὸ Χριστοῦ [Ἰησοῦ]. 13 ἀδελφοί, ἐγὼ ἐμαυτὸν οὐ³ λογίζομαι κατειληφέναι· ᵃἓν δέ, τὰ μὲν ὀπίσω ἐπιλανθανόμενος τοῖς δὲ ἔμπροσθεν ἐπεκτεινόμενος, 14ᵃ κατὰ σκοπὸν διώκω εἰς τὸ βραβεῖον τῆς ἄνω κλήσεως τοῦ θεοῦ ἐν Χριστῷ Ἰησοῦ. 15 Ὅσοι οὖν τέλειοι, τοῦτο φρονῶμεν· καὶ εἴ τι ἑτέρως φρονεῖτε, καὶ τοῦτο ὁ θεὸς ὑμῖν ἀποκαλύψει· 16 πλὴν εἰς ὃ ἐφθάσαμεν, τῷ αὐτῷ στοιχεῖν⁴.

17 Συμμιμηταί μου γίνεσθε, ἀδελφοί, καὶ σκοπεῖτε

---

² 12 {B} ἔλαβον ἢ ἤδη τετελείωμαι p⁶¹ᵛⁱᵈ ℵ A B Dᶜ K P Ψ 33 81 88 (104 τεθέαμαι) 181 326 330 436 451 614 629 630 1241 1739 1877 1881 1962 1984 (1985 omit ἢ ἤδη) 2127 2492 2495 Byz itᶜ,ᵈᵉᵐ,ᵈⁱᵛ,ˣ,ᶻ vg syrᵖ,ʰ copˢᵃ,ᵇᵒ goth arm Clement Tertullian Origenˡᵃᵗ Eusebius Victorinus-Rome Hilary // ἔλαβον ἢ ἤδη δεδικαίωμαι ἢ ἤδη τετελείωμαι (see 1 Cor 4.4?) (p⁴⁶ τελείωμαι) D* (G for δεδικαίομαι as alternative τετελείωμαι) itᵃʳ,ᵈ,ᵉ,ᶠ,(ᵍ) Irenaeusˡᵃᵗ Ambrosiaster // τετελείωμαι itᵗ

³ 13 {C} οὐ p⁴⁶ B Dᶜ G K Ψ 88 181 326 630 1739 1877 1881 2495 Byz itᶜ,ᵈ,ᵈᵉᵐ,ᵈⁱᵛ,ᵉ,ᶠ,ᵍ,ˣ,ᶻ vg syrᵖ,ʰ copˢᵃ arm Origenˡᵃᵗ Victorinus-Rome Ephraem Chrysostom Jerome¹/² // οὔπω p¹⁶ᵛⁱᵈ,⁶¹ᵛⁱᵈ ℵ A Dᵍʳ* P 33 81 104 330 436 451 614 (629 transposes: οὔπω ἐμαυτόν) 1241 1962 1984 1985 2127 2492 itᵃʳ syrʰ ʷⁱᵗʰ * copᵇᵒ goth eth Clement Tertullian Ambrosiaster Basil Chrysostom Jerome¹/² Euthalius Theodoret Cosmas Antiochus Paschal Chronicle John-Damascus

⁴ 16 {B} τῷ αὐτῷ στοιχεῖν p¹⁶,¹⁶ ℵ* A B Iᵛⁱᵈ 33 424ᶜ 1739 copˢᵃ,ᵇᵒ ethʳᵒ Hilary Augustine Theodotus-Ancyra Ferrandus // τὸ αὐτὸ φρονεῖν 1881 // τὸ αὐτὸ φρονεῖν, τῷ αὐτῷ στοιχεῖν (D)* τῷ αὐτοι [sic]) (G συνστοιχεῖν) itᵃʳ,ᵈ,ᵉ,ᵍ Ambrosiaster Victorinus-Rome // τὸ αὐτὸ φρονεῖν, τῷ αὐτῷ κανόνι στοιχεῖν (Dᶜ 436 στοιχεῖν κανόνι) 81 104 330 451 (629 φρονεῖν καὶ τῷ) 1241 2127 2492 itᶜ,ᵈᵉᵐ,ᵈⁱᵛ,ᶠ,ˣ,ᶻ vg goth arm Euthalius // τῷ αὐτῷ στοιχεῖν κανόνι, τὸ αὐτὸ φρονεῖν ℵᶜ K P Ψ 88 181 326 424* 614 630 1877 1962 1984 1985 2495 Byz syrᵖ,ʰ ethᵖᵖ Chrysostom Theodore Theodoret John-Damascus // τῷ αὐτῷ κανόνι στοιχεῖν, τὸ αὐτὸ φρονεῖν 69 1908

ᵃ ᵃ 13-14 a no number, a number 14: TRᵉᵈ WH Bov BF² AV RV ASV RSV NEB Zür Luth Jer Seg // a number 14, a no number: TRᵉᵈ

---

12 διώκω...καταλάβω 1 Tm 6.12, 19 κατελήμφθην...Ἰησοῦ Ac 9.5-6 14 1 Cor 9.24
15 Ὅσοι...φρονῶμεν Mt 5.48; 1 Cor 2.6 16 Ga 6.16 17 Συμμιμηταί μου γίνεσθε
1 Cor 4.16; 11.1 σκοπεῖτε...ἡμᾶς 1 Th 1.7; 1 Pe 5.3

Moving Ever Forward

12 Not that I have reached it yet or have already attained perfection,* but I am in pursuit, in the hope that somehow I may get it in my grasp,ª since I too have been grasped* by Christ [Jesus]. 13 My brethren, I do not consider myself to have it already in my grasp, but I can at least say that I give no thought to what lies behind but strain toward that which lies ahead; 14 I hold my attention on the goal as I run toward the prize[b]—God's calling me ever upward in Christ Jesus.

15 All of us then who have been initiated* must take this attitude. If in any point you think otherwise, God will clarify that for you also. 16 Only, we must stand firmly by that which we have already attained.*

Christ Our Goal

17 My brethren, join together in following my example,[c]* and observe the behavior of those who conduct them-

τοὺς οὕτω περιπατοῦντας καθὼς ἔχετε τύπον ἡμᾶς. 18 πολλοὶ γὰρ περιπατοῦσιν οὓς πολλάκις ἔλεγον ὑμῖν, νῦν δὲ καὶ κλαίων λέγω, τοὺς ἐχθροὺς τοῦ σταυροῦ τοῦ Χριστοῦ, 19 ὧν τὸ τέλος ἀπώλεια, ὧν ὁ θεὸς ἡ κοιλία καὶ ἡ δόξα ἐν τῇ αἰσχύνῃ αὐτῶν, οἱ τὰ ἐπίγεια φρονοῦντες. 20 ἡμῶν γὰρ τὸ πολίτευμα ἐν οὐρανοῖς ὑπάρχει, ἐξ οὗ καὶ σωτῆρα ἀπεκδεχόμεθα κύριον Ἰησοῦν Χριστόν, 21 ὃς μετασχηματίσει τὸ σῶμα τῆς ταπεινώσεως ἡμῶν σύμμορφον τῷ σώματι τῆς δόξης αὐτοῦ κατὰ τὴν ἐνέργειαν τοῦ δύνασθαι αὐτὸν καὶ ὑποτάξαι αὐτῷ[5] τὰ πάντα.

4 Ὥστε, ἀδελφοί μου ἀγαπητοὶ καὶ ἐπιπόθητοι, χαρὰ καὶ στέφανός μου, οὕτως στήκετε ἐν κυρίῳ, ἀγαπητοί.

Exhortations

2 Εὐοδίαν παρακαλῶ καὶ Συντύχην παρακαλῶ τὸ αὐτὸ φρονεῖν ἐν κυρίῳ. 3 ναὶ ἐρωτῶ καὶ σέ, γνήσιε σύζυγε[a], συλλαμβάνου αὐταῖς, αἵτινες ἐν τῷ εὐαγγελίῳ συνήθλησάν μοι μετὰ καὶ Κλήμεντος καὶ τῶν λοιπῶν συνεργῶν μου[1], ὧν τὰ ὀνόματα ἐν βίβλῳ ζωῆς. 4 Χαίρετε ἐν κυρίῳ πάντοτε· πάλιν ἐρῶ, χαίρετε. 5 τὸ ἐπιεικὲς ὑμῶν γνωσθήτω πᾶσιν ἀνθρώποις. ὁ κύριος ἐγγύς.[b]

---

[5] 21 {B} αὐτῷ B³ K 33 88 330 451 614 629 1739 1877 1881 1962 1984 1985 2127 2492 2495 Byz^pt Lect it^{d,e,g} syr^{p,h} cop^{sa?bo?} Eusebius Victorinus-Rome Epiphanius Chrysostom Cyril Euthalius // αυτω ℵ* A B* D* G P // ἑαυτῷ ℵ^c D^c Ψ 104 181 326 436 630 1241 Byz^pt l^{598,599} it^{ar,c,dem,div,f,x,z} vg arm Hilary Ambrose Chrysostom Theodoret John-Damascus

[1] 3 {B} τῶν λοιπῶν συνεργῶν μου p^{46} ℵ^c A B D G I^{vid} K P Ψ 33 81 88 104 181 326 330 436 451 614 629 630 1241 1739 1877 1881 1962 1984 1985 2127 2492 2495 Byz Lect it^{ar,c,d,dem,div,e,f,g,x,z} vg syr^{p,h} cop^{sa,bo} goth arm Origen Eusebius // τῶν συνεργῶν μου καὶ τῶν λοιπῶν p^{16vid} ℵ*

[a] 3 σύζυγε: TR WH Bov BF² AV RV ASV RSV NEB Zür^{mg} Luth (Jer) Seg // Σύζυγε: WH^{mg} Zür (Jer)

[b] 5 b major: TR Bov BF² AV RV ASV RSV Zür Luth Jer Seg // b minor: WH NEB

18 τούς...Χριστοῦ 1 Cor 1.23; Ga 6.12 19 ὧν ὁ θεὸς ἡ κοιλία Ro 16.18 οἱ τὰ ἐπίγεια φρονοῦντες Ro 8.5–6 20 ἡμῶν...ὑπάρχει Eph 2.6, 19; He 12.22 21 ὃς μετασχηματίσει... αὐτόν Ro 8.29; 1 Cor 15.43–53 ὑποτάξαι...πάντα 1 Cor 15.28

4 1 ἀδελφοί...μου 1 Th 2.19–20 3 βίβλῳ ζωῆς Ex 32.32, 33; Ps 69.28; Dn 12.1; Re 3.5; 13.8; 17.8; 20.12, 15; 21.27 4 Php 3.1 5 ὁ κύριος ἐγγύς He 10.37; Jas 5.8, 9

selves according to the pattern you have in us. 18 For alas many go about in a manner which shows them to be enemies of the cross of Christ,ᵃ as I have often said to you, this time with tears in my eyes. 19 These people will end up in disaster! Their god is the stomach;ᵇ their "glory" is in their very shamefulness.★ I mean those people who are preoccupied with things of this world.ᶜ 20 But our citizen-rights are in Heaven,ᵈ★ and it is from there that we await expectantly the coming of our savior, the Lord Jesus Christ. 21 He will give a new form to this lowly body of ours, making it into an image of his own glorified body,ᵉ in exercise of that power by which he can actually bring the whole universe into subjection to himself.ᶠ

V. THE CHALLENGE OF VIRTUE

■ CHAPTER FOUR ■

Christian Concord

1 For these reasons, my brethren whom I so love and long for, you who are my joy and crown,ᵍ continue as now to stand firm in the Lord, dearly beloved. 2 I plead with Evodia and Syntyche: come to a mutual understanding in the Lord. 3 Yes, and I ask you also, my true fellow-worker,★ go to their aid, for they have struggled at my side in promoting the Gospel, along with Clement★ and my other co-workers—all of whose names are in the Book of Life.ʰ

Joy and Peace

4 Rejoice in the Lord always;ⁱ I will say it again: rejoice! 5 All men should notice how agreeable you are. The Lord is near.ʲ

6 μηδὲν μεριμνᾶτε, ἀλλ᾽ ἐν παντὶ τῇ προσευχῇ καὶ τῇ δεήσει μετὰ εὐχαριστίας τὰ αἰτήματα ὑμῶν γνωριζέσθω πρὸς τὸν θεόν.ᶜ 7 καὶ ἡ εἰρήνη τοῦ θεοῦ ἡ ὑπερέχουσα πάντα νοῦν φρουρήσει τὰς καρδίας ὑμῶν καὶ τὰ νοήματα ὑμῶν ἐν Χριστῷ Ἰησοῦ.

8 Τὸ λοιπόν, ἀδελφοί, ὅσα ἐστὶν ἀληθῆ, ὅσα σεμνά, ὅσα δίκαια, ὅσα ἁγνά, ὅσα προσφιλῆ, ὅσα εὔφημα, εἴ τις ἀρετὴ καὶ εἴ τις ἔπαινος, ταῦτα λογίζεσθε· 9 ἃ καὶ ἐμάθετε καὶ παρελάβετε καὶ ἠκούσατε καὶ εἴδετε ἐν ἐμοί, ταῦτα πράσσετε· καὶ ὁ θεὸς τῆς εἰρήνης ἔσται μεθ᾽ ὑμῶν.

Acknowledgment of the Philippians' Gift

10 Ἐχάρην δὲ ἐν κυρίῳ μεγάλως ὅτι ἤδη ποτὲ ἀνεθάλετε τὸ ὑπὲρ ἐμοῦ φρονεῖν, ἐφ᾽ ᾧ καὶ ἐφρονεῖτε, ἠκαιρεῖσθε δέ. 11 οὐχ ὅτι καθ᾽ ὑστέρησιν λέγω, ἐγὼ γὰρ ἔμαθον ἐν οἷς εἰμι αὐτάρκης εἶναι. 12 οἶδα καὶ ταπεινοῦσθαι, οἶδα καὶ περισσεύειν· ἐν παντὶ καὶ ἐν πᾶσιν μεμύημαι, καὶ χορτάζεσθαι καὶ πεινᾶν καὶ περισσεύειν καὶ ὑστερεῖσθαι· 13 πάντα ἰσχύω ἐν τῷ ἐνδυναμοῦντί με. 14 πλὴν καλῶς ἐποιήσατε συγκοινωνήσαντές μου τῇ θλίψει.

15 Οἴδατε δὲ καὶ ὑμεῖς, Φιλιππήσιοι, ὅτι ἐν ἀρχῇ τοῦ εὐαγγελίου, ὅτε ἐξῆλθον ἀπὸ Μακεδονίας, οὐδεμία μοι ἐκκλησία ἐκοινώνησεν εἰς λόγον δόσεως καὶ λήμψεως εἰ μὴ ὑμεῖς μόνοι, 16 ὅτι καὶ ἐν Θεσσαλονίκῃ καὶ ἅπαξ καὶ δὶς εἰς τὴν χρείαν μοι[2] ἐπέμψατε. 17 οὐχ ὅτι ἐπιζητῶ

---

[2] 16 {C} εἰς τὴν χρείαν μοι ℵ B G^ur K Ψ 33 88 181 1739 1877 1881 2127 2495 *Byz Lect* it^(c,d,dem,div,e,f,x,z^c) vg ∥ εἰς τὴν χρείαν μου D^c P 614 629 630 1962 1984 1985 it^(ar),r² ∥ τὴν χρείαν μοι p⁴⁶ A 81 104 326 330 436 451 1241 2492

ᶜ 6 c major: TR Bov BF² AV RV ASV RSV NEB Jer Seg ∥ c minor: WH ∥ c exclamation: Zür Luth

6 μηδὲν μεριμνᾶτε Mt 6.25; 1 Pe 5.7   τῇ προσευχῇ...εὐχαριστίας Col 4.2   7 Is 26.3; Jn 14.27; Col 3.15   8 Ro 12.17   9 ὁ θεὸς τῆς εἰρήνης Ro 15.33; 16.20; 1 Cor 14.33; 1 Th 5.23   11 ἐν...εἶναι 1 Tm 6.6   13 2 Cor 12.10; 2 Tm 4.17   15 2 Cor 11.9

6 Put all anxiety away from your minds.ª Present your needs to God in every form of prayer and in petitions full of gratitude.ᵇ 7 Then will God's own peace,ᶜ which goes beyond all comprehension, stand guard over your hearts and minds, in Christ Jesus.

8 Finally, my brethren, your thoughts should be wholly directed to all that is true, whatever deserves respect, everything that is honest, pure, lovely, decent, virtuous, worthy of praise.ᵈ★ 9 Live according to what you have learned and accepted from me, what you have heard me saying and have seen me doing.★ Then will the God of peaceᵉ be with you.

Generosity

10 It was a deep joy to me in the Lord that at last your concern for me blossomed forth once more. You had been concerned, of course; but lacked the opportunity.

Accommodations to Circumstances

11 Not that I say this because I am in want; for whatever the situation I find myself in, I have learned to be self-sufficient. 12 Just as I am experienced in being brought low, so also I know what it is to have an abundance. I have learned the secret for every type of circumstance—how to eat well and how to go hungry, how to have abundance and how to go without.ᶠ 13 I have strength for anything, in him who is the source of all my strength!ᵍ

Gratitude

14 Still, it was good of you to share with me in my hardships. 15 You yourselves know, my dear Philippians, that at the start of my evangelizing,★ when I left Macedonia, not a single congregation shared with me by way of giving something for what it had received—except you alone.ʰ 16 For instance, even when I was at Thessalonike you sent something for my needs, not only once but twice. 17 It is not, of

τὸ δόμα, ἀλλὰ ἐπιζητῶ τὸν καρπὸν τὸν πλεονάζοντα εἰς λόγον ὑμῶν. 18 ἀπέχω δὲ πάντα καὶ περισσεύω· πεπλήρωμαι δεξάμενος παρὰ Ἐπαφροδίτου τὰ παρ' ὑμῶν, ὀσμὴν εὐωδίας, θυσίαν δεκτήν, εὐάρεστον τῷ θεῷ. 19 ὁ δὲ θεός μου πληρώσει πᾶσαν χρείαν ὑμῶν κατὰ τὸ πλοῦτος αὐτοῦ ἐν δόξῃ ἐν Χριστῷ Ἰησοῦ. 20 τῷ δὲ θεῷ καὶ πατρὶ ἡμῶν ἡ δόξα εἰς τοὺς αἰῶνας τῶν αἰώνων, ἀμήν.

Final Greetings

21 Ἀσπάσασθε πάντα ἅγιον ἐν Χριστῷ Ἰησοῦ. ἀσπάζονται ὑμᾶς οἱ σὺν ἐμοὶ ἀδελφοί. 22 ἀσπάζονται ὑμᾶς πάντες οἱ ἅγιοι, μάλιστα δὲ οἱ ἐκ τῆς Καίσαρος οἰκίας. 23 ἡ χάρις τοῦ κυρίου Ἰησοῦ Χριστοῦ μετὰ τοῦ πνεύματος ὑμῶν.[3]

[261?] syr[h] goth eth ∥ τὴν χρείαν μου D[gr*] arm Ambrosiaster Augustine ∥ μοι εἰς τὴν χρείαν μου (syr[p]) cop[sa,bo] ∥ in unum mihi it[z*] ∥ in necessitatem meam vel usibus meis it[g]

[3] 23 {B} ὑμῶν. B G 1881 it[f,g] cop[sa] Victorinus-Rome Ambrosiaster Chrysostom Euthalius ∥ ὑμῶν. ἀμήν. p[46] ℵ A D K L P Ψ 33 81 88 104 181 326 330 436 451 614 629 630 1241 1739 1877 1962 1984 1985 2127 2492 2495 Byz Lect it[ar,c,d,dem,div,e,r2,x,z] vg syr[p,h] cop[bo] arm eth Theodoret John-Damascus

---

17 ἐπιζητῶ τόν...ὑμῶν 1 Cor 9.11   18 ὀσμὴν εὐωδίας Gn 8.21; Ex 29.18; Eze 20.41
22 οἱ ἐκ...οἰκίας Php 1.13

course, that I am eager for the gift; rather, I am eager for the ever-growing credits which accrue to your account. **18** Here is my receipt that I have now been fully paid, and beyond. I am very well supplied because of what I received from you through Epaphroditus, "a fragrant offering,"ᵃ★ an acceptable sacrifice, pleasing to God.

Recompense

19 My God in turn will fully supply whatever you need, in a manner befitting his magnificent riches in Christ Jesus.

20 All glory for unending ages to our God and Father!ᵇ Amen.

VI. FAREWELL

21 Give my greetings in Christ Jesus to every believer.★ My brothers here send their greetings to you, **22** as do all the faithful, particularly those in Caesar's service.ᶜ **23** May the favor of the Lord Jesus Christ be with your spirit!

Explanatory Notes

1.1: Paul usually at the start of his letters refers to himself as "apostle of Jesus Christ". Here he substitutes "slave" (implying that he is unconditionally obligated to the service of Christ), probably because in view of the situation at Philippi he wishes to stress his fellow-servant status rather than emphasize his apostolic authority. The reference to Timothy here is a courtesy; Paul alone writes the letter—as use of the singular verb throughout shows, as also the reference in 2.19-24 to Timothy in the third person.

1.1: "Sanctified": literally, "saints", but not in the later technical sense. So also, "leaders and assistants" (episkopoi and diakonoi) do not yet have their specific meaning of "bishops" and "deacons" as they came soon to signify (cp. use at Ti 1.5-7, Acts 6.1-6; 14.23; 20.17,28; 1 pt 5.2).

1.2: Note that the blessing comes from Christ the Lord, not just through him from the Father.

1.3: "recall"—sc. in prayer, reminding God of you and your needs.

1.9: Their love of God and of fellow-Christians will grow as they become more sensitive to recognizing God's goodness in all that they experience.

1.10: "The day of Christ": the Parousia, triumphant return of Christ, when those loyal to him will be with him and share in his eternal glory (cp.1.6; 2.16; 2 Thes 2.4; 1 Thes 4.17; 5.10; 1 Cor 1.8).

1.12: "brethren" (adelphoi) is idiomatic for all his 'kin in Christ', all fellow-believers of the Gospel; it includes women as well as men (cp.4.3).

1.13: "official guard" (Praitorion) refers to the garrison of the Governor of a Province (here likely Ephesus, where inscriptions referring to a Praetorion have been found), like that of the Imperial Guard at Rome itself.

1.19: "turn out to my salvation", an echo of Job 13.16, hoping that God will turn his suffering to his ultimate good and deliverance from evil.

1.20: His imprisonment clearly implies a threat to his life.

1.21: "living is Christ", that is, the opportunity to preach Christ and serve him; death is "a profit" because it means full union with Christ, and release from the struggles of this imperfect life (cp.2 Cor 5.2-8; Col 3.3).

1.26: "being with you again". Acts 20.1,6 records subsequent visits to Philippi.

1.30: This refers to his imprisonment at Philippi (Acts 16.19-24; 1 Thes 2.2), and to his present confinement—probably at Ephesus (cp. 2 Cor 1.8-10; 7.5).

2.5: The following passage (6-11) is apparently a Christological hymn of the early Church, well known to Paul's converts. (Other hymns seem echoed at 1 Tim 3.16; Col 1.15-20; Heb 1.3-4). The language is un-Pauline in many words and formulations, there is a rhythmic parallelism to the structure resembling the Psalms, the two long sentences break into three stanzas each (the first triad stressing Christ, the second God: Christ's divine pre-existence, his humiliation by incarnation, and further humiliation by death; God's glorifying him, subjecting to him the whole universe, and re-affirming his divine dignity as Lord). Paul seems to have added the central phrase between the two halves ("yes, death on a cross!"), one of his favorite Christological themes. In any case, whether Paul composed this splendid tribute to Christ or is quoting it, he fully adopts all its profound theological concepts.

2.6: "usurpation": something seized by force, not possessed by right. Christ has by his nature all the divine prerogatives. Others take this word (harpagmon) in the sense of "something to grasp, hold on to, cling to, refuse to give up".

2.7: "dispossessed himself": he put aside not his inalienable divinity but the privilege of divine glory which was his right and which his Father would restore to him in reward for his selfless redemptive sacrifice (cp. Jn 17.5: "Father, now give me glory at your side, the glory I had with you before the world began"). The word (ekenosen) is commonly translated "emptied" himself.

2.7: "condition of a slave": in total submission to his Father's will and plan for our redemption. There is an echo of the Suffering Servant of Yahweh in Isaiah 53, a fore-type of the Messiah.

2.7: "in the likeness of men": fully human, and seen as such. Cp. Jn 1.1,14: "the Word was with God, and was God...and became flesh and dwelt among us."

2.8: "death on a cross": this is the ultimate humiliation from the state of divine glory, the nadir of Christ's self-abasement.

2.9: "name": in Jewish and other ancient cultures, the name reveals and expresses the nature, essence of what is named.

2.10: "every knee must bend": this echoes Is 45.23 where Yahweh proclaims "to me every knee shall bend"—thus indicating the divine dignity of Christ the Lord.

2.12: "anxious concern": literally, "with fear and trembling"—a common Old Testament expression instilling awe and seriousness into the service of God (cp. Ex 15.16; Is 19.16; Ps 2.11; Jdt 2.28).

2.16: "hold toward it" as a lamp enlightening the unbelieving world's darkness. Some translate this word (epechontes) as "hold fast".

2.17: "libation": in ancient religious ritual, the pouring out on the ground of a liquid offering as a sacrifice. Paul means that he may be facing death.

2.24: "I will come again": cp. note on 1.26

3.1: "rejoice": the word (chairete) is also used in the sense of "welcome" and "farewell", but that is unlikely here, in view of Paul's repeated stress on joy in this epistle, and the addition of "always" in its parallel use at 4.4.

3.2: "mutilation": a sarcastic play on words—(katome) here echoing (peritome) (circumcision) in the next sentence, and associating it with the self-inflicted mutilations of the prophets of Baal (1 Kgs 18.28) and of devotees of Cybele who slashed themselves in religious frenzy. Cp. Gal 5.12.

3.3: "we are the Circumcision": the true people of God, "seed and offering of Abraham" (Gal 3.7, 29; 6.15).

3.3: "Spirit of God": some MSS read "worship God by the Spirit."

3.5: "circumcised on the eighth day": as the Law imposed (Gn 17.12; Lv 12.3).

3.5: "Pharisee": publicly committed to strict observance of the whole Law of Moses.

3.7: "liability": knowledge of Christ has led Paul to re-assess, re-evaluate the ways of truly pleasing and serving God. An indication of the profound and lasting effect of his overwhelming experience of the reality and meaning of Christ on the way to Damascus some 20 years before. It is not mere intellectual knowledge.

3.9: The contrast between these two ways to please God is the main theme of Paul's epistles to the Romans and to the Galatians, where the topic is more fully developed.

3.12: "attained perfection": this may be an echo of the concept in the ancient Mystery Religions of being an initiate (teleios: perfected), admitted to divine secrets.

3.12: "grasped by Christ": Paul was a prize pursued by Christ, the 'Hound of Heaven', until captured outside Damascus (Acts 9.1-22). The purpose of Christ in giving Paul the grace of that profound conversion and illumination was that he might share in Christ's suffering and resurrection.

3.15: "initiated": see note 3.12 above.

3.16: Some MSS add, probably to explain Paul's cryptic phrase, "thinking alike."

3.17: "following my example": this is not arrogance, but humble simplicity, since all his converts know that Paul is wholly dedicated to imitating Christ (1 Cor 11.1; cp. also Phil 4.9; 1 Thes 1.6; 2 Thes 3.7,9; 1 Cor 4.6).

3.19: "shamefulness": probably referring to their circumcised sexual organ.

3.20: "citizen-rights in Heaven": M. Dibelius nicely says "Our true home is Heaven; here on earth we are a colony of citizens from Heaven."

4.3: "fellow-worker": referring to some prominent helper of Paul in the Philippian community. Or it may be a proper name, Syzygus—which fits the parallelism better.

4.3: This Clement is identified by Eusebius in his history of the early Church as Pope Clement, third successor of Peter at Rome.

4.8: These virtues were commonly praised by the Greek philosophers, but Paul gives them new motivation: the imitation of Christ.

4.9: Paul's example: see note on 3.17.

4.15: "start of my evangelizing": it was at Philippi that Paul first preached Christ in Europe, going on from there to Thessalonike and Beroea (Acts 16.9-17.14).

4.18: "fragrant offering": an allusion to a frequent phrase in the Old Testament: Ex 29.18; Ez 20.41; Gn 8.21; Lv 1.9,13, etc.

4.21: "believer", like "faithful" in the next verse, is what "saints" (Paul's word here) means in context, as also at 1.1: persons consecrated to God by faith and loyalty.

Cross-References

Page 9

a Rom 1.7; Gal 1.3; Phlm 3
b 1 Thes 1.2; 1 Cor 1.4
c Phil 2.13
d Phil 1.10; 2.16; 1 Cor 1.8
e Rom 1.9; 2 Cor 1.23; 1 Thes 2.5
f Col 1.9-10; Phlm 6
g Rom 2.18; 12.2; Heb 5.14
h Phil 1.6; 2.16; 1 Cor 1.8
i Jn 15.8

Page 11

a Eph 3.1; 6.20; 2 Tim 2.9; Phlm 1, 9
b Job 13.16
c 2 Cor 1.11
d 1 Pt 4.16; 1 Cor 6.20
e Gal 2.20

Page 13

a Rom 1.13
b 2 Cor 5.8
c Eph 4.1; Col 1.10; 1 Thes 2.12
d Phil 4.3
e Acts 5.41; Mt 5.10; 10.38; Mk 8.34; Lk 9.23
f Phil 1.13
g Rom 15.5; 1 Cor 1.10

Page 15

a Gal 5.26
b Rom 12.3, 10
c 1 Cor 10.24,33; 13.5
d Jn 1.1; 17.5; Heb 1.3; Col 2.9
e 2 Cor 8.9
f Jn 1.14; Rom 8.3; Heb 2.14, 17; Gal 4.4; Is 53.3
g Jn 10.17; Heb 5.8; 12.2; Mt 26.39
h Acts 2.33
i Heb 1.3-4; Eph 1.21
j Rom 14.11; Is 45.23; Jn 5.23; Rv 5.13
k Acts 2.36; Rom 10.9; 1 Cor 12.3; Col 2.6

Page 17

a Ps 2.11
b Jn 15.5; 1 Cor 12.6; 15.10; 2 Cor 3.5
c 1 Cor 10.10; 1 Pt 4.9

d Mt 10.16; Acts 2.40; Dt 32.5
e Mt 5.14; Eph 5.8; Dn 12.3
f 1 Thes 2.19
g Is 49.4; 65.23; Gal 2.2
h 2 Tim 4.6
i Phil 3.1; 4.4
j 1 Cor 4.17; 16.10; Acts 16.1-3; 17.14-15
k 2 Tim 4.10

Page 19

a Phil 4.18
b 1 Cor 16.18
c Phil 2.18; 4.4

Page 21

a Ps 22.16, 20; Rv 22.15; 2 Cor 11.13
b Rom 2.29
c 2 Cor 11.18, 21-23
d Lk 1.59; 2.21
e 2 Cor 11.22
f Acts 22.3; 23.6; 26.5
g Acts 8.3; 22.4; 26.9-11
h Mt 13.44, 46; Lk 14.33
i Rom 3.21-22
j Rom 6.3-5; 8.17; Gal 6.17
k Acts 4.2; Rv 20.5-6; Jn 11.25-26

Page 23

a 1 Tim 6.12, 19
b 1 Cor 9.24-25; 2 Tim 4.7
c 1 Cor 4.16; 11.1; 1 Pt 5.3; 1 Thes 1.7

Page 25

a Gal 6.12; 1 Cor 1.23
b Rom 16.18
c Rom 8.5-6
d Eph 2.6, 19; Col 3.1-3; Heb 12.22; 2 Cor 5.4-5
e Rom 8.23, 29; 1 Cor 15.43-53; 2 Cor 3.18; 5.1-5
f 1 Cor 15.28; Eph 4.6; Col 3.11
g 1 Thes 2.19-20
h Ex 32.32-33; Ps 69.28; Dn 12.1; Lk 10.20; Rv 3.5; 13.8; 17.8; 20.12,15; 21.27
i Phil 2.18; 3.1
j Heb 10.37; Jas 5.8-9

Page 27

a Mt 6.25; 1Pt 5.7
b Col 4.2
c Jn 14.27; Col 3.15
d Rom 12.17
e Rom 15.33; 16.20; 1 Cor 14.33; 1 Thes 5.23
f 1 Cor 4.11; 2 Cor 6.10; 11.27
g 2 Cor 12.9-10; 2 Tm 4.17
h 2 Cor 11.9; 1 Cor 9.11

Page 29

a Gn 8.21; Ex 29.18
b Eph 5.20; 1 Thes 1.3; 3.11, 13; Mt 6.9
c Phil 1.13

ΠΡΟΣ ΓΑΛΑΤΑΣ

Introduction

Salient features of Paul's personality and theological teaching are vividly clear in this powerful plea to his converts from paganism to stand firm in their acceptance of Christ and his redemptive suffering as the only source of spiritual salvation, replacing the Mosaic Law as the true way to God. Interesting details of Paul's life are also learned here, and a graphic insight into the problems of the early Church and its relation to Judaism.

The epistle was probably written around 54 or 55 A.D., most likely from Ephesus after Paul's arrival there for several years' stay on his third missionary journey (*Acts* 19, + 20.31). The Galatians to whom it was addressed were Paul's converts among the descendants of earlier Kelts who had invaded western and central Asia Minor long before and had settled in the territory around Ancyra (modern Ankara). Paul had passed through this area on his second missionary journey (see *Acts* 16.6 and 18.23). It is less likely that the recipients of this vehement letter were his churches in the southern regions of Pisidia, Lycaonia, and Pamphylia where he had preached earlier in the Hellenized cities of Perge, Iconium, Pisidian Antioch, Lystra, and Derbe, though this area was sometimes considered part of larger Galatia and some scholars think it the destination of this epistle. In any case, the new Christians whom Paul is addressing were converts from paganism now being enticed by other missionaries to adopt also the basic observances of the Jewish Law.

Clearly, since Paul's visit some other interpretation of Christianity had been brought to these neophytes, probably by converts from Judaism (perhaps from the austere Essene sect) who insisted on the necessity of still following the Mosaic Law along with their new faith in Christ. They were undermining Paul's authority also, implying that he had not been trained by Christ himself like the original apostles, that he had hidden from his converts in Galatia the necessity of accepting circumcision and other key obligations of the Jewish Law, in order to win them more easily to Christ, and that his gospel was not the full and authentic one.

When Paul learned of this, he was stirred to write this impassioned defense of his apostolic authority, his correct understanding of the faith, the unique importance of Christ and his redemptive sacrifice on the cross, the freedom which Christians enjoy from the old burdens of the Law, the total sufficiency of Christ as the way to God and eternal life, and the beauty of spiritual rebirth through faith in Christ and the new life of the Spirit. *Galatians* is a summary of basic Pauline theology. Its themes were more fully developed in Paul's later great letter to the Romans.

In his vigorous stress on the absolute preeminence of Christ and his cross as God's way to salvation and holiness, Paul sometimes exaggerates the ineffectiveness of the Mosaic Law as a means to gain divine favor and blessings. The pious Jew saw in the Law a way established by God himself to win divine approval by a life of meticulous observance of ritual, social, and moral obligations. Paul's profound insight into the higher designs of God in Christ led him to understand and welcome the priority of faith and the supernatural gifts of the Spirit. His enthusiasm for this new vision of the life of grace in Christ and of the uniquely salvific role of Christ's redemptive death on the cross irradiates this whole epistle.

The contents of the epistle divide into: I Introduction (1.1-10), II Paul's Defense of his Authority and Doctrine (1.11—2.21), III Christian Faith and Liberty (3.1—4.31), IV Exhortation to Christian Living (5.1—6.10), V Conclusion (6.11-18).

The Greek text is reprinted from *The Greek New Testament*, edited by Aland, Black, Martini, Metzger, and Wickgren, third edition,* by permission of the publisher, United Bible Societies. The textual notes at the bottom of each page indicate manuscript variants. Explanatory notes to the content are provided, and references to parallel passages elsewhere in Scripture and identification of the location of Old Testament citations.

* (corrected)

ΠΡΟΣ ΓΑΛΑΤΑΣ

Salutation

1 Παῦλος ἀπόστολος οὐκ ἀπ᾽ ἀνθρώπων οὐδὲ δι᾽ ἀνθρώπου ἀλλὰ διὰ Ἰησοῦ Χριστοῦ καὶ θεοῦ πατρὸς τοῦ ἐγείραντος αὐτὸν ἐκ νεκρῶν, 2 καὶ οἱ σὺν ἐμοὶ πάντες ἀδελφοὶ ταῖς ἐκκλησίαις τῆς Γαλατίας, 3 χάρις ὑμῖν καὶ εἰρήνη ἀπὸ θεοῦ πατρὸς ἡμῶν καὶ κυρίου[1] Ἰησοῦ Χριστοῦ 4 τοῦ δόντος ἑαυτὸν ὑπὲρ τῶν ἁμαρτιῶν ἡμῶν, ὅπως ἐξέληται ἡμᾶς ἐκ τοῦ αἰῶνος τοῦ ἐνεστῶτος πονηροῦ κατὰ τὸ θέλημα τοῦ θεοῦ καὶ πατρὸς ἡμῶν, 5 ᾧ ἡ δόξα εἰς τοὺς αἰῶνας τῶν αἰώνων, ἀμήν.

There is No Other Gospel

6 Θαυμάζω ὅτι οὕτως ταχέως μετατίθεσθε ἀπὸ τοῦ καλέσαντος ὑμᾶς ἐν χάριτι [Χριστοῦ][2] εἰς ἕτερον εὐαγγέλιον,[a] 7 ὃ οὐκ ἔστιν ἄλλο,[a] εἰ μή τινές εἰσιν οἱ

---

[1] 3 {C} πατρὸς ἡμῶν καὶ κυρίου ℵ A P Ψ 33 81 (181 ὑμῶν) 326 1241 1962 2127 *l*⁵⁹⁸ it^(ar,c,x) Ambrosiaster Ambrose^(1/2) Chrysostom Maximinus^(acc. to Augustine) Augustine Euthalius // πατρὸς καὶ κυρίου ἡμῶν 𝔓^(46,51vid) B D G H K 88 104 330 436 451 614 629 630 1739 1881 1984 1985 2492 2495 *Byz Lect* it^(d,dem,e,f,g,z) vg syr^(p,h,pal) cop^(sa,bo^ms) goth arm Victorinus-Rome Ambrose^(1/2) Jerome Augustine Theodoret // πατρὸς καὶ κυρίου 1877 (Varimadum) Pelagius Chrysostom Augustine Vigilius John-Damascus // πατρὸς ἡμῶν καὶ κυρίου ἡμῶν cop^(bo) eth

[2] 6 {D} Χριστοῦ 𝔓⁵¹ ℵ A B K P Ψ 33 81 88 104 181 330 436 451 614 629 630 1739 1877 1881 1962 1984 1985 2127 2492 2495 *Byz Lect* it^(dem,f,x) vg syr^(p,h,pal) cop^(bo) goth arm Eusebius Basil Euthalius // Ἰησοῦ Χριστοῦ D 326 1241 *l*⁵⁹⁹ it^(d,e) syr^(h with *) // Χριστοῦ Ἰησοῦ it^(z) cop^(sa) Jerome // θεοῦ 7 327 336 Origen^(lat) Theodoret // *omit* 𝔓^(46vid) G H^(vid) it^(ar,g) Marcion Tertullian Cyprian Ambrosiaster Victorinus-Rome Lucifer Ephraem Pelagius

---

a a 6-7 a minor, a minor: Zür // a minor, a major: WH Bov BF² RV ASV Luth // a major, a minor: TR AV (ASV^(mg)) NEB Seg // a dash, a minor: RSV Jer

1 ἀπόστολος...Χριστοῦ Ga 1.11-12; Ac 20.24   3 Ro 1.7; Php 1.2; Phm 3   4 τοῦ δόντος ...ἁμαρτιῶν ἡμῶν Ga 2.20; 1 Tm 2.6; Tt 2.14   τοῦ αἰῶνος...πονηροῦ 1 Jn 5.19   7 τινές...ὑμᾶς Ac 15.24

■ CHAPTER ONE ■

I. INTRODUCTION

Greeting

1 Paul, an apostle not sent by any group of men acting for any man, but by commission★ of Jesus Christ[a] and of God his Father who raised him from the dead, 2 and all my brethren★ who are with me, to the churches in Galatia: 3 may you have favor and peace from God our Father and from the Lord Jesus Christ[b] 4 who sacrificed himself for our sins[c] that he might rescue us from the midst of today's evil world,[d]★ in accord with the will of our Father—5 to whom be all glory for endless ages, Amen.

Reproof for Disloyalty

6 I am amazed that so soon you are deserting★ him who graciously called you,★ and going over to another gospel[c]— 7 not that there is any other,★ but someone must have unsettled

ταράσσοντες ὑμᾶς καὶ θέλοντες μεταστρέψαι τὸ εὐαγγέλιον τοῦ Χριστοῦ. 8 ἀλλὰ καὶ ἐὰν ἡμεῖς ἢ ἄγγελος ἐξ οὐρανοῦ εὐαγγελίζηται [ὑμῖν]³ παρ᾽ ὃ εὐηγγελισάμεθα ὑμῖν, ἀνάθεμα ἔστω. 9 ὡς προειρήκαμεν καὶ ἄρτι πάλιν λέγω, εἴ τις ὑμᾶς εὐαγγελίζεται παρ᾽ ὃ παρελάβετε, ἀνάθεμα ἔστω. 10 Ἄρτι γὰρ ἀνθρώπους πείθω ἢ τὸν θεόν; ἢ ζητῶ ἀνθρώποις ἀρέσκειν; εἰ ἔτι ἀνθρώποις ἤρεσκον, Χριστοῦ δοῦλος οὐκ ἂν ἤμην.

How Paul Became an Apostle

11 Γνωρίζω γὰρ ὑμῖν, ἀδελφοί, τὸ εὐαγγέλιον τὸ εὐαγγελισθὲν ὑπ᾽ ἐμοῦ ὅτι οὐκ ἔστιν κατὰ ἄνθρωπον· 12 οὐδὲ γὰρ ἐγὼ παρὰ ἀνθρώπου παρέλαβον αὐτὸ οὔτε ἐδιδάχθην ἀλλὰ δι᾽ ἀποκαλύψεως Ἰησοῦ Χριστοῦ.

13 Ἠκούσατε γὰρ τὴν ἐμὴν ἀναστροφήν ποτε ἐν τῷ Ἰουδαϊσμῷ, ὅτι καθ᾽ ὑπερβολὴν ἐδίωκον τὴν ἐκκλησίαν τοῦ θεοῦ καὶ ἐπόρθουν αὐτήν, 14 καὶ προέκοπτον ἐν τῷ Ἰουδαϊσμῷ ὑπὲρ πολλοὺς συνηλικιώτας ἐν τῷ γένει μου, περισσοτέρως ζηλωτὴς ὑπάρχων τῶν πατρικῶν μου παραδόσεων. 15 ὅτε δὲ εὐδόκησεν [ὁ θεὸς]⁴ ὁ ἀφορίσας

---

³ 8 {D} εὐαγγελίζηται ὑμῖν Dᶜ (Dᵍʳ* 330 451 2492 ὑμᾶς) 33 (1962 ἡμῖν) 1984 2127 Byzᵖᵗ *l*⁶⁰³ itᵈᵉᵐ,ᶠ,ˣ,ᶻ vg syrᵖ?ʰ?ᵖᵃˡ? copˢᵃ?ᵇᵒ? Chrysostom Theodoret ∥ ὑμῖν εὐαγγελίζηται pʰˡᵛⁱᵈ B H 630 1739 Archelaus ∥ εὐαγγελίζεται ὑμῖν K P 88 (104 εὐαγγελίσεται) 181 436 614 629 1877 1881 1985 2495 Byzᵖᵗ Lect syrᵖ?ʰ?ᵖᵃˡ? copˢᵃ?ᵇᵒ? Theodoret ∥ εὐαγγελίσηται ὑμῖν ℵᶜ A 81 326 (1241 ἡμῖν) itᵈ,ᵉ syrᵖ?ʰ?ᵖᵃˡ? copˢᵃ?ᵇᵒ? arm Tertullian Adamantius Eusebius Ambrosiaster Epiphanius (Athanasius Cyril-Jerusalem John-Damascus ὑμᾶς) ∥ ἄλλως εὐαγγελίσηται Marcion Cyprian ∥ εὐαγγελίζηται (Gᵍʳ* εὐαγγελιζαηται [sic]) Ψ itᵃʳ Cyprian Eusebius Basil ∥ εὐαγγελίσηται ℵ* itᵍ Tertullian Victorinus-Rome Lucifer Cyril

⁴ 15 {D} εὐδόκησεν (or ηὐδόκησεν) ὁ θεός ℵ A D K P Ψ 33 81 88 104 181 326 330 436 451 614 630 1241 1739 1877 1881 1962 1984 1985 2127 2492 Byz Lect itᵈ,ᵉ syrʰ ʷⁱᵗʰ *, ᵖᵃˡ copˢᵃ,ᵇᵒ arm eth Irenaeusˡᵃᵗ Origenᵍʳ,ˡᵃᵗ Adamantius

---

7 θέλοντες...Χριστοῦ Ac 15.1   8, 9 ἀνάθεμα ἔστω 1 Cor 16.22   10 Ἄρτι...θεόν 1 Th 2.4
12 Ga 1.1   13 ἐδίωκον...αὐτήν Ac 8.3; 22.4-5; 26.9-11   14 Ac 22.3   15 ὁ ἀφορίσας... καλέσας Is 49.1; Jr 1.5; Ro 1.1

you,ᵃ wishing to overturn the Gospel of Christ. 8 Now, even if we or an angel from heaven should preach [to you] a gospel not in accord with the Gospel we preached to you, reject him with curses!ᵇ³★ 9 Once more I repeat what I have already said: if anyone tries to teach you a gospel other than the one you learned, reject him with curses!

10 Whose favor am I courting now—men's or God's?ᶜ Is this how I 'seek to ingratiate myself with men'?★ If I were still trying to win men's approval,★ I would not be Christ's servant!

II. PAUL'S DEFENSE OF HIS AUTHORITY AND DOCTRINE

His Call by Christ

11 My brethren, I want you to realize that the Gospel whose good news I brought to you is no human invention.ᵈ 12 I did not myself receive it from any man or human teacher, but by revelation from Jesus Christ.ᶜ★ 13 You have heard, I know, the story of my former way of life in Judaism. You know that I persecuted the Church of Godᶠ beyond all measure and tried to destroy it; 14 that I made progress in the Jewish observances far beyond many of my age and generation, since I was more than others an unrestrained zealot for living out all the traditions from my forefathers.ᵍ 15 But the time came when He★ who had set me apart "before I was

με εκ κοιλίας μητρός μου και καλέσας διά της χάριτος αυτού 16 αποκαλύψαι τον υιόν αυτού εν εμοί, ίνα ευαγγελίζωμαι αυτόν εν τοις έθνεσιν, ευθέως ου προσανεθέμην σαρκί και αίματι 17 ουδέ ανήλθον εις Ιεροσόλυμα προς τους προ εμού αποστόλους, αλλά απήλθον εις Αραβίαν και πάλιν υπέστρεψα εις Δαμασκόν.

18 Έπειτα μετά έτη τρία ανήλθον εις Ιεροσόλυμα ιστορήσαι Κηφάν και επέμεινα προς αυτόν ημέρας δεκαπέντε, 19 έτερον δε των αποστόλων ουκ είδον ει μη Ιάκωβον τον αδελφόν του κυρίου. 20 ά δε γράφω υμίν, ιδού ενώπιον του θεού ότι ου ψεύδομαι. 21 έπειτα ήλθον εις τα κλίματα της Συρίας και της Κιλικίας· 22 ήμην δε αγνοούμενος τω προσώπω ταις εκκλησίαις της Ιουδαίας ταις εν Χριστώ. 23 μόνον δε ακούοντες ήσαν ότι Ο διώκων ημάς ποτε νυν ευαγγελίζεται την πίστιν ην ποτε επόρθει, 24 και εδόξαζον εν εμοί τον θεόν.

Paul Accepted by the Other Apostles

2 Έπειτα διά δεκατεσσάρων ετών πάλιν ανέβην[1] εις Ιεροσόλυμα μετά Βαρναβά συμπαραλαβών και Τίτον· 2 ανέβην δε κατά αποκάλυψιν· και ανεθέμην αυτοίς το ευαγγέλιον ό κηρύσσω εν τοις έθνεσιν, κατ' ιδίαν δε

Eusebius Epiphanius Chrysostom Severian Jerome Augustine Cyril Euthalius Theodoret Vigilius Ps-Athanasius John-Damascus ∥ *ευδόκησεν* p[46] B G 629 2495 it[ar,dem,f,g,x,z] vg syr[p,h] Irenaeus[lat] (Origen) Eusebius Ambrosiaster Victorinus-Rome Faustinus[acc. to Augustine] Epiphanius Gaudentius Chrysostom Jerome Theodoret

[1] 1 {B} *πάλιν ανέβην* p[46] ℵ A B K P Ψ (33* *ανέβη*) 33[c] 81 88 104 181 326 330 436 451 614 629 630 1241 1739 1877 1881 1962 1984 1985 2127 2492 2495 *Byz Lect* it[dem,f,x,z] vg syr[(p),h] cop[sa] arm ∥ *πάλιν ανήλθον* C Paschal Chronicle ∥ *ανέβην πάλιν* D G it[ar,d,e,g] goth eth Pelagius Jerome ∥ *ανέβην* it[c] cop[bo] Marcion Irenaeus[lat] Tertullian Ambrosiaster Chrysostom Augustine

16 αποκαλύψαι...εμοί Ac 9.3–6; 22.6–10; 26.13–18   ίνα...έθνεσιν Ga 2.7   18 Ac 9.26
19 Ιάκωβον...κυρίου Mt 13.55; Mk 6.3   20 Ac 9.30
2 1 Ac 15.2

born" and had "called" me★ by his favorᵃ 16 chose to reveal his Son within me,ᵇ★ that I might spread the good news of him among the Gentiles.ᶜ Immediately, without seeking to consult human advisers★ 17 or even going to Jerusalem to see those who were apostles before me, I went off into Arabia,★ then later returned to Damascus. 18 Then, three years later, I went up to Jerusalem to get to know Kephas,★ staying with him fifteen days. 19 I did not see any other of the apostles; I only saw James the kinsman of the Lord.ᵈ★ 20 I protest before God that what I have just written to you is the truth.

21 Thereafter I went into the districts of Syria and Cilicia.★ 22 Christ's churches in Judaea did not even know what I looked like; 23 they only kept hearing that 'he who once was persecuting us is now preaching the very faith he used to be trying to demolish,' 24 and they gave glory to God on my account.

■ CHAPTER TWO ■

The Council of Jerusalem

1 Then after fourteen years I again went up to Jerusalem★ with Barnabas,ᶜ also taking along Titus.★ 2 Now I went as a result of a revelation★ and I laid out for their examination the Gospel as I present it to the Gentiles—but in private conference

τοῖς δοκοῦσιν, μή πως εἰς κενὸν τρέχω ἢ ἔδραμον. 3 ἀλλ' οὐδὲ Τίτος ὁ σὺν ἐμοί, Ἕλλην ὤν, ἠναγκάσθη περιτμηθῆναι· 4 διὰ δὲ τοὺς παρεισάκτους ψευδαδέλφους, οἵτινες παρεισῆλθον κατασκοπῆσαι τὴν ἐλευθερίαν ἡμῶν ἣν ἔχομεν ἐν Χριστῷ Ἰησοῦ, ἵνα ἡμᾶς καταδουλώσουσιν,ᵃ 5 οἷς οὐδὲ² πρὸς ὥραν εἴξαμεν τῇ ὑποταγῇ, ἵνα ἡ ἀλήθεια τοῦ εὐαγγελίου διαμείνῃ πρὸς ὑμᾶς. 6 ἀπὸ δὲ τῶν δοκούντων εἶναί τι,—ᵇ ὁποῖοί ποτε ἦσαν οὐδέν μοι διαφέρει· πρόσωπον [ὁ] θεὸς ἀνθρώπου οὐ λαμβάνει —ᵇ ἐμοὶ γὰρ οἱ δοκοῦντες οὐδὲν προσανέθεντο, 7 ἀλλὰ τοὐναντίον ἰδόντες ὅτι πεπίστευμαι τὸ εὐαγγέλιον τῆς ἀκροβυστίας καθὼς Πέτρος τῆς περιτομῆς, ᶜ8 ὁ γὰρ ἐνεργήσας Πέτρῳ εἰς ἀποστολὴν τῆς περιτομῆς ἐνήργησεν καὶ ἐμοὶ εἰς τὰ ἔθνη,ᶜ 9 καὶ γνόντες τὴν χάριν τὴν δοθεῖσάν μοι, Ἰάκωβος καὶ Κηφᾶς καὶ Ἰωάννης, οἱ δοκοῦντες στῦλοι εἶναι, δεξιὰς ἔδωκαν ἐμοὶ καὶ Βαρναβᾷ κοινωνίας, ἵνα ἡμεῖς εἰς τὰ ἔθνη, αὐτοὶ δὲ εἰς τὴν περιτομήν· 10 μόνον τῶν πτωχῶν ἵνα μνημονεύωμεν, ὃ καὶ ἐσπούδασα αὐτὸ τοῦτο ποιῆσαι.

---

² 5 {B} οἷς οὐδέ p⁴⁶ ℵ A B C Dᶜ G K P Ψ 33 81 88 104 181 326 330 436 451 614 629 630 1241 1739 1877 1881 1962 1984 1985 2127 2492 2495 *Byz Lect* itᵃʳ,ᵈᵉᵐ,ᶠ,ᵍ,ˣ,ᶻ vg syrʰ copˢᵃ,ᵇᵒ goth arm (eth) Marcion Greek mssᵃᶜᶜ· to Ambrosiaster, Victorinus-Rome Basil Ambrose Ps-Ignatius Epiphanius Chrysostom Pelagius Greek mssᵃᶜᶜ· to Jerome Jerome Theodoreˡᵃᵗ Augustine Euthalius Theodoret Ps-Jerome Cassiodorus John-Damascus // οὐδέ syrᵖ Marcion Greek mssᵃᶜᶜ· to Ambrosiaster Ephraem // οἷς mssᵃᶜᶜ· to Primasius, Sedulius // *omit* D* itᵈ,ᵉ Irenaeusˡᵃᵗ Tertullian Ambrosiaster Greek and Latin mssᵃᶜᶜ· to Victorinus-Rome Victorinus-Rome Pelagius Latin mssᵃᶜᶜ· to Jerome Augustine Primasius Latin mssᵃᶜᶜ· to Cassiodorus, Claudius

ᵃ 4 *a* minor: TR Bov BF² AV RV ASV NEB Luth Jer // *a* dash: WH RSV Zür // *a* ellipsis: Seg

ᵇᵇ 6 *b* dash, *b* dash: WH Bov BF² Zür Luth Jer Seg // *b* parens, *b* parens: AV RV ASV RSV // *b* parens, *b* parens and dash: NEB // *b* minor, *b* major: TR

ᶜᶜ 8 *c c* no dashes or parens: TR WH Bov BF² NEB // *c* parens, *c* parens: AV RV ASV RSV // *c* dash, *c* dash: Zür Luth Jer Seg

4 διὰ...ψευδαδέλφους Ac 15.1, 24; Ga 1.7   τὴν ἐλευθερίαν...Χριστῷ Ga 5.1, 13
6 πρόσωπον...λαμβάνει Dt 10.17   7 πεπίστευμαι...ἀκροβυστίας Ac 9.15; 22.21
10 Ac 11.29-30

with the leaders,* to check on whether possibly I was following or had been following a course leading nowhere. 3 Now not even Titus who was there with me was ordered to undergo circumcision, Greek though he is. 4 It* was all on account of certain so-called brothers who had furtively slipped in, insinuating themselves into the group to spy on the freedom that is ours in Christ Jesus and to make slaves of us.ᵃ 5 Not for a moment did we yield to their oppression.* This was in order that the truth of the Gospel should survive intact for your benefit. 6 However those who were regarded as important (and it makes no difference to me what kind of men they once were—God does not play favorites* among menᵇ)—the leaders, I say, made me add nothing.* 7 On the contrary, recognizing that I have been entrusted with the Gospel for the pagansᶜ just as Peter has been for the Jews* 8 (for He who made Peter effective for the apostolate among the Jews had also been at work in me for the benefit of the Gentiles) 9 and recognizing the favor bestowed on me, the admitted pillars—James and Kephas and John—gave me and Barnabas the handclasp of fellowship, on the understanding that we should go to the Gentiles and they themselves to the Jews, 10 the only proviso being that we should be mindful of the poor—the very thing that I made every effort to do.

Paul Rebukes Peter at Antioch

11 Ὅτε δὲ ἦλθεν Κηφᾶς εἰς Ἀντιόχειαν, κατὰ πρόσωπον αὐτῷ ἀντέστην, ὅτι κατεγνωσμένος ἦν. 12 πρὸ τοῦ γὰρ ἐλθεῖν τινας³ ἀπὸ Ἰακώβου μετὰ τῶν ἐθνῶν συνήσθιεν· ὅτε δὲ ἦλθον⁴, ὑπέστελλεν καὶ ἀφώριζεν ἑαυτὸν φοβούμενος τοὺς ἐκ περιτομῆς. 13 καὶ συνυπεκρίθησαν αὐτῷ [καὶ] οἱ λοιποὶ Ἰουδαῖοι, ὥστε καὶ Βαρναβᾶς συναπήχθη αὐτῶν τῇ ὑποκρίσει. 14 ἀλλ' ὅτε εἶδον ὅτι οὐκ ὀρθοποδοῦσιν πρὸς τὴν ἀλήθειαν τοῦ εὐαγγελίου, εἶπον τῷ Κηφᾷ ἔμπροσθεν πάντων, Εἰ σὺ Ἰουδαῖος ὑπάρχων ἐθνικῶς καὶ οὐχὶ Ἰουδαϊκῶς ζῇς, πῶς τὰ ἔθνη ἀναγκάζεις Ἰουδαΐζειν;

Jews, like Gentiles, are Saved by Faith

15 Ἡμεῖς φύσει Ἰουδαῖοι καὶ οὐκ ἐξ ἐθνῶν ἁμαρτωλοί·ᵈ 16 εἰδότες [δὲ] ὅτι οὐ δικαιοῦται ἄνθρωπος ἐξ ἔργων νόμου ἐὰν μὴ διὰ πίστεως Ἰησοῦ Χριστοῦ, καὶ ἡμεῖς εἰς Χριστὸν Ἰησοῦν ἐπιστεύσαμεν, ἵνα δικαιωθῶμεν ἐκ πίστεως Χριστοῦ καὶ οὐκ ἐξ ἔργων νόμου, ὅτι ἐξ ἔργων νόμου οὐ δικαιωθήσεται πᾶσα σάρξ. 17 εἰ δὲ ζητοῦντες δικαιωθῆναι ἐν Χριστῷ εὑρέθημεν καὶ αὐτοὶ ἁμαρτωλοί, ἆρα Χριστὸς ἁμαρτίας διάκονος; μὴ γένοιτο.

---

³ 12 {A} τινας ℵ A B C D^gr G H^vid K P Ψ 33 81 88 104 181 326 330 436 451 614 629 630 1241 1739 1877 1881 1962 1984 1985 2127 2492 2495 Byz Lect it^ar,dem,f,g*,r1 c ,x,z vg syr^p,h cop^sa,bo goth arm Origen Ambrosiaster Victorinus-Rome Chrysostom Pelagius Euthalius John-Damascus // τινα p⁴⁶ it^d,e,g^c,r1* Irenaeus

⁴ 12 {B} ἦλθον A C D^c H K P Ψ 81 88 104 181 326 436 614 629 630 1241 1739 1877 1881 1962 1984 1985 2127 2495 Byz Lect it^ar,dem,f,r1 c,x,z vg syr^p,h cop^sa,bo goth arm Ambrosiaster Victorinus-Rome Chrysostom Euthalius John-Damascus // ἦλθεν p⁴⁶ ℵ B D* G 33 330 451 2492 it^d,e,g,r1* Irenaeus Origen Pelagius

---

ᵈ 15 d major: NEB Luth Jer Seg // d minor: TR WH Bov BF² AV RV ASV RSV Zür

---

12 μετά...συνήσθιεν Ac 11.3   16 οὐ δικαιοῦται...σάρξ Ac 15.10, 11; Ro 3.20, 28; 4.5; 11.6; Eph 2.8; Ga 3.11   οὐ δικαιωθήσεται πᾶσα σάρξ Ps 143.2

Peter's Conciliation of the Judaizers

11 So too, when Kephas came to Antioch, I confronted him personally,* that he stood self-condemned.* 12 For he had been taking his meals with the Gentiles^a* before the arrival of certain followers of James. When they came however, he began to draw back* and to segregate himself, seeking to avoid those who insisted on circumcision.* 13 Then the other Jews also joined in his dissembling, to the point that even Barnabas was swept away by their hypocrisy.* 14 Now when I observed that they were not walking straight toward the truth of the Gospel, I spoke in the presence of all to Kephas: "If you who are a Jew are living according to Gentile ways rather than Jewish, by what logic do you force the Gentiles to adopt Jewish ways?"

Paul's Basic Stand

15 "We are Jews by birth [I continued*], not sinners from among the Gentiles.* 16 Knowing that no one is justified except by faith in Jesus Christ—not by legal observances^b— we too* have put our faith in Christ Jesus, in order to be justified by faith in Christ and not by observances of the Law, since *no man will be justified** by observances of the Law.

17 Now if in seeking to be justified in Christ we ourselves turn out to be sinful,* does that mean that Christ is encouraging sin? Impossible!

18 εἰ γὰρ ἃ κατέλυσα ταῦτα πάλιν οἰκοδομῶ, παραβάτην ἐμαυτὸν συνιστάνω. 19 ἐγὼ γὰρ διὰ νόμου νόμῳ ἀπέθανον, ἵνα θεῷ ζήσω. ᵉΧριστῷ συνεσταύρωμαι· 20ᵉ ζῶ δὲᶠ οὐκέτι ἐγώ, ζῇ δὲ ἐν ἐμοὶ Χριστός· ὃ δὲ νῦν ζῶ ἐν σαρκί, ἐν πίστει ζῶ τῇ τοῦ υἱοῦ τοῦ θεοῦ⁵ τοῦ ἀγαπήσαντός με καὶ παραδόντος ἑαυτὸν ὑπὲρ ἐμοῦ. 21 οὐκ ἀθετῶ τὴν χάριν τοῦ θεοῦ· εἰ γὰρ διὰ νόμου δικαιοσύνη, ἄρα Χριστὸς δωρεὰν ἀπέθανεν.

Law or Faith

3 Ὦ ἀνόητοι Γαλάται, τίς ὑμᾶς ἐβάσκανεν, οἷς κατ' ὀφθαλμοὺς Ἰησοῦς Χριστὸς προεγράφη ἐσταυρωμένος; 2 τοῦτο μόνον θέλω μαθεῖν ἀφ' ὑμῶν· ἐξ ἔργων νόμου τὸ πνεῦμα ἐλάβετε ἢ ἐξ ἀκοῆς πίστεως; 3 οὕτως ἀνόητοί ἐστε, ἐναρξάμενοι πνεύματι νῦν σαρκὶ ἐπιτελεῖσθε; 4 τοσαῦτα ἐπάθετε εἰκῇ; εἴ γε καὶ εἰκῇ. 5 ὁ οὖν ἐπιχορηγῶν ὑμῖν τὸ πνεῦμα καὶ ἐνεργῶν δυνάμεις ἐν ὑμῖν, ἐξ ἔργων νόμου ἢ ἐξ ἀκοῆς πίστεως; 6 καθὼς Ἀβραὰμ **ἐπίστευσεν τῷ θεῷ, καὶ ἐλογίσθη αὐτῷ εἰς δικαιοσύνην.**

7 Γινώσκετε ἄρα ὅτι οἱ ἐκ πίστεως, οὗτοι υἱοί εἰσιν Ἀβραάμ. 8 προϊδοῦσα δὲ ἡ γραφὴ ὅτι ἐκ πίστεως δικαιοῖ τὰ ἔθνη ὁ θεός, προευηγγελίσατο τῷ Ἀβραὰμ ὅτι **Ἐνευλογηθήσονται ἐν σοὶ πάντα τὰ ἔθνη·** 9 ὥστε

---

⁵ 20 {B} υἱοῦ τοῦ θεοῦ ℵ A C Dᶜ K P Ψ 33 81 88 104 181 326 436 451 614 629 630 1241 1739 1877 1881 1962 1984 2127 2492 2495 *Byz Lect* itᵃʳ·ᵈᵉᵐ· ᶠ·ʳ¹·ᵗ·ˣ·ᶻ vg syrᵖ·ʰ copˢᵃ·ᵇᵒ goth arm eth Clement Adamantius Ambrosiaster Chrysostom Jerome Augustine Cyril Euthalius Theodoret John-Damascus ∥ θεοῦ τοῦ υἱοῦ 1985 ∥ θεοῦ καὶ Χριστοῦ 𝔭⁴⁶ B D* G itᵈ·ᵉ·ᵍ Victorinus-Rome Pelagius ∥ θεοῦ 330

ᵉ ᵉ 19-20 *e* no number, *e* number 20: TRᵉᵈ WH? Bov BF² Zür Luth Jer Seg ∥ *e* number 20, *e* no number: TRᵉᵈ WH? AV RV ASV RSV NEB

ᶠ 20 ƒ none: TR WH BF² RVᵐᵍ ASV RSV NEB Seg ∥ ƒ minor: Bov AV RV Zür Luth Jer

---

19 νόμῳ ἀπέθανον Ro 7.6 20 τοῦ υἱοῦ...με Jn 13.1; 17.23; 1 Jn 3.16 παραδόντος...ἐμοῦ Ga 1.4; 1 Tm 2.6; Tt 2.14
3 6 ἐπίστευσεν...δικαιοσύνην Gn 15.6 (Ro 4.3) 8 Ἐνευλογηθήσονται...ἔθνη Gn 12.3 (18.18; Sir 44.21; Ac 3.25) 9 Ro 4.16

18 For surely I prove myself a transgressor when I build up again the very things I had torn down!* 19 In fact, it was in obedience to the Law that I died in regard to the Law,ᵃ* in order to live for God. I have been crucified along with Christ, 20 and it is no longer I who live but Christ living in me.* Insofar as I now live in the body, I live in faith in the Son of God who loved me and gave himself up for me.ᵇ* 21 I will not treat God's gracious gift* as meaningless!* Clearly, if justice comes through the Law, then Christ died for nothing!"ᶜ

III. CHRISTIAN FAITH AND LIBERTY

■ CHAPTER THREE ■

Faith is the Source of Justification

1 My Galatians! Are you out of your minds?* Who has cast a spell* upon you? You, before whose eyes Jesus Christ was displayed to view* upon his cross! 2 Answer me one question: how did you receive the Spirit? Through observance of the Law, or through believing what you heard? 3 Can you possibly be so foolish? After starting off spiritually, are you now going to seek fulfillment in the flesh?* 4 Are all your many experiences in vain? If indeed they were merely in vain!* 5 Does He who lavished the Spirit upon you and works wonders in your midst* do so then because you observe the Law, or because you believed what you heard? 6 Take the case of Abraham: *he believed God and it was credited to him as justice.*ᵈ* 7 See what this means: it is they who believe who are sons of Abraham!* 8 Because Scripture saw in advance that God's way of justifying the Gentiles is through faith, it foretold this good news to Abraham: *All nations shall*

οἱ ἐκ πίστεως εὐλογοῦνται σὺν τῷ πιστῷ Ἀβραάμ. 10 ὅσοι γὰρ ἐξ ἔργων νόμου εἰσίν, ὑπὸ κατάραν εἰσίν· γέγραπται γὰρ ὅτι **Ἐπικατάρατος πᾶς ὃς οὐκ ἐμμένει πᾶσιν τοῖς γεγραμμένοις ἐν τῷ βιβλίῳ τοῦ νόμου τοῦ ποιῆσαι αὐτά.** 11 ὅτι δὲ ἐν νόμῳ οὐδεὶς δικαιοῦται παρὰ τῷ θεῷ δῆλον, ὅτι **Ὁ δίκαιος ἐκ πίστεως ζήσεται**· 12 ὁ δὲ νόμος οὐκ ἔστιν ἐκ πίστεως, ἀλλ᾽ **Ὁ ποιήσας αὐτὰ ζήσεται ἐν αὐτοῖς.** 13 Χριστὸς ἡμᾶς ἐξηγόρασεν ἐκ τῆς κατάρας τοῦ νόμου γενόμενος ὑπὲρ ἡμῶν κατάρα,[a] ὅτι γέγραπται, **Ἐπικατάρατος πᾶς ὁ κρεμάμενος ἐπὶ ξύλου,**[a] 14 ἵνα εἰς τὰ ἔθνη ἡ εὐλογία τοῦ Ἀβραὰμ γένηται ἐν Χριστῷ Ἰησοῦ, ἵνα τὴν ἐπαγγελίαν[1] τοῦ πνεύματος λάβωμεν διὰ τῆς πίστεως.

The Law and the Promise

15 Ἀδελφοί, κατὰ ἄνθρωπον λέγω· ὅμως ἀνθρώπου κεκυρωμένην διαθήκην οὐδεὶς ἀθετεῖ ἢ ἐπιδιατάσσεται. 16 τῷ δὲ Ἀβραὰμ ἐρρέθησαν αἱ ἐπαγγελίαι καὶ τῷ σπέρματι αὐτοῦ. οὐ λέγει, Καὶ τοῖς σπέρμασιν, ὡς ἐπὶ πολλῶν ἀλλ᾽ ὡς ἐφ᾽ ἑνός, **Καὶ τῷ σπέρματί σου,** ὅς ἐστιν Χριστός. 17 τοῦτο δὲ λέγω· διαθήκην προκεκυρωμένην ὑπὸ τοῦ θεοῦ[2] ὁ μετὰ τετρακόσια καὶ τριάκοντα

[1] 14 {B} ἐπαγγελίαν ℵ A B C D^c K P Ψ 33 81 88^mk 104 181 330 436 451 614 629 630 1241 1739 1877 1881 1962 1984 2127 2492 2465 Byz Lect it^(ar,c,dem,f,(r1),x,z) vg syr^(p,h,pal) cop^(sa,bo) arm Origen Ambrosiaster Jerome Augustine // εὐλογίαν (see 3.14a) p^46 D* F^gr G 88* it^(d,e,g,t) Marcion Ambrosiaster Ephraem Vigilius

[2] 17 {B} θεοῦ p^46 ℵ A B C P Ψ 33 81 330 436 451 1241 1739 1881 2492 it^(dem,f,r1,x,z) vg cop^(sa,bo) eth Aphraates Ephraem Jerome Augustine Cyril Euthalius John-Damascus // θεοῦ εἰς Χριστόν D^gr G^gr I K 0176 88 104 181 614 629 630 1877 1962 1984 1985 2127 2495 Byz Lect arm Chrysostom Theo-

[a a] 13 a minor, a minor: TR WH Bov BF² AV RV ASV Luth Jer // a minor, a major: NEB // a dash, a dash: RSV Zür Seg

10 Ἐπικατάρατος...αὐτά Dt 27.26   11 ἐν...θεῷ Ro 3.20; Ga 2.16   Ὁ δίκαιος...ζήσεται Hab 2.4 (Ro 1.17; He 10.38)   12 Ὁ ποιήσας...αὐτοῖς Lv 18.5 (Ro 10.5)   13 Χριστὸς... νόμου Ro 8.3; Ga 4.5   γενόμενος...κατάρα 2 Cor 5.21   Ἐπικατάρατος...ξύλου Dt 21.23   16 Καὶ τῷ σπέρματί σου Gn 12.7; 13.15; 17.7; 24.7   17 τετρακόσια...ἔτη Ex 12.40

be blessed in you.★ **9** That is to say, all believers are blessed along with Abraham the man of faith.ᵃ★

The Law Does Not Cause Justification

10 On the other hand, all who depend on observance of the Law are threatened by a curse, for it is written: *Cursed is every man who does not abide by everything written in the Book of the Law and carry it out.*★ **11** Again, it is obvious that no one is justified in God's sight by the Law,ᵇ for *the just man will live because of his faith.*★ **12** Now the Law is not dependent on faith; rather, *whoever observes* these things *will find life through them.*★ **13** Christ has purchased us back from the Law's curseᶜ by becoming for our sakes a curse,★ as it is written: *Cursed is every man who is hanged on a tree.*★ **14** The purpose of all this was to extend upon the Gentiles, in Christ Jesus, the blessing bestowed on Abraham, to make it possible for us★ to receive, through faith, the Spirit promised us.

The Law Did Not Nullify the Promise to Abraham

15 My brethren, let me put my argument in terms of human practice: no one can set aside or add to even a man's★ last will once duly validated.ᵈ **16** Now the Promises★ were spoken to Abraham "and to his descendant."★ It is not said "and to his descendants," as applicable to many, but in a way applicable to one only: *and to your descendant*, that is, Christ. **17** This is my point: a covenant formally ratified by God★ is not set aside as no longer valid, to the extent of rendering the Promise null and void, by the Law that came into being four hundred and thirty years later.ᶜ

ἔτη γεγονὼς νόμος οὐκ ἀκυροῖ εἰς τὸ καταργῆσαι τὴν ἐπαγγελίαν. 18 εἰ γὰρ ἐκ νόμου ἡ κληρονομία, οὐκέτι ἐξ ἐπαγγελίας· τῷ δὲ Ἀβραὰμ δι' ἐπαγγελίας κεχάρισται ὁ θεός. 19 Τί οὖν ὁ νόμος; τῶν παραβάσεων χάριν προσετέθη, ἄχρις οὗ ἔλθῃ τὸ σπέρμα ᾧ ἐπήγγελται, διαταγεὶς δι' ἀγγέλων[b] ἐν χειρὶ μεσίτου. 20 ὁ δὲ μεσίτης ἑνὸς οὐκ ἔστιν, ὁ δὲ θεὸς εἷς ἐστιν.

Slaves and Sons

21 Ὁ οὖν νόμος κατὰ τῶν ἐπαγγελιῶν [τοῦ θεοῦ][3]; μὴ γένοιτο. εἰ γὰρ ἐδόθη νόμος ὁ δυνάμενος ζῳοποιῆσαι, ὄντως ἐκ νόμου ἂν ἦν ἡ δικαιοσύνη· 22 ἀλλὰ συνέκλεισεν ἡ γραφὴ τὰ πάντα ὑπὸ ἁμαρτίαν, ἵνα ἡ ἐπαγγελία ἐκ πίστεως Ἰησοῦ Χριστοῦ δοθῇ τοῖς πιστεύουσιν.

23 Πρὸ τοῦ δὲ ἐλθεῖν τὴν πίστιν ὑπὸ νόμον ἐφρουρούμεθα συγκλειόμενοι εἰς τὴν μέλλουσαν πίστιν ἀποκαλυφθῆναι, 24 ὥστε ὁ νόμος παιδαγωγὸς ἡμῶν γέγονεν εἰς Χριστόν, ἵνα ἐκ πίστεως δικαιωθῶμεν· 25 ἐλθούσης δὲ τῆς πίστεως οὐκέτι ὑπὸ παιδαγωγόν ἐσμεν.[c]

26 Πάντες γὰρ υἱοὶ θεοῦ ἐστε διὰ τῆς πίστεως ἐν Χριστῷ Ἰησοῦ· 27 ὅσοι γὰρ εἰς Χριστὸν ἐβαπτίσθητε, Χριστὸν ἐνεδύσασθε. 28 οὐκ ἔνι Ἰουδαῖος οὐδὲ Ἕλλην,

---

dore[lat] Theodoret Paschal Chronicle Theophylact ∥ θεοῦ ἐν Χριστῷ it[ar.d.e.g] syr[p.h] Ambrosiaster Pelagius

[3] 21 {C} τοῦ θεοῦ ℵ A C D[gr] (G omit τοῦ) K P Ψ 33 81 88 181 330 436 451 614 629 630 1241 1739 1877 1881 1962 1984 1985 2127 2492 2495 Byz Lect it[ar,dem,f,g,r¹,x,z] vg syr[p.h.pal] cop[sa,bo] arm Chrysostom Jerome Augustine Cyril Euthalius Theodoret John-Damascus ∥ τοῦ Χριστοῦ 104 ∥ omit p[46] B it[d.e] Ambrosiaster Victorinus-Rome

---

[b] 19 b none: TR WH AV RV ASV RSV Zür Luth ∥ b minor: Bov BF² NEB (Jer) Seg

[c] 25-26 c major: TR WH Bov BF² AV RV ASV NEB Luth Zür Jer Seg ∥ c minor: RSV

---

18 εἰ...ἐξ ἐπαγγελίας Ro 4.14; 11.6   19 Τί...προσετέθη Ro 5.20   διαταγεὶς δι' ἀγγέλων Ac 7.38, 53; He 2.2   21 Ὁ οὖν...γένοιτο Ro 8.2–4   22 συνέκλεισεν...ἁμαρτίαν Ro 3.11–19; 11.32   23 ὑπὸ νόμον ἐφρουρούμεθα Ga 4.3   24 Ro 10.4   26 Jn 1.12   27 εἰς Χριστὸν ἐβαπτίσθητε Ro 6.3   Χριστὸν ἐνεδύσασθε Ro 13.14   28 οὐκ...Ἕλλην Ro 10.12

18 Clearly, if the inheritance comes by virtue of the Law, it is no longer conferred by virtue of the Promise.[a]★ Yet it was by way of the Promise that God granted Abraham his privilege.

The Law's True Function

19 Why, then, the Law? It was provided as a supplement in view of transgressions of it,[b]★ until that Descendant came to whom the Promise had been given. It was promulgated by the help of angels★ and through the services of a mediator.★ 20 Now there can be no mediator when only one person is involved—and God is only one.★ 21 Is the Law, then, in opposition to the Promises [of God]? Impossible![c] Obviously, if the Law which was given were such as could impart life, righteousness would in reality be a consequence of the Law.★ 22 On the contrary, Scripture has locked in all things under subjection to sin.[d]★ Why? That the Promise, as a fruit of faith in Jesus Christ, might be given to those who believe.

What Faith Has Brought Us

23 Now before the faith came we were held in custody under the law,[e] locked in until the faith that was coming should be revealed. 24 In other words, the Law functioned as our guide★ to Christ,[f] that we might come to justification through faith. 25 But with the faith now here, we are no longer in the attendant's charge. 26 You are all, in fact, sons★ of God[g] because of your faith, in union with Christ Jesus. 27 Yes, all of you who have been baptized into Christ have clothed yourselves with Christ;[h]★ 28 there is not now

οὐκ ἔνι δοῦλος οὐδὲ ἐλεύθερος, οὐκ ἔνι ἄρσεν καὶ θῆλυ· πάντες γὰρ ὑμεῖς εἷς ἐστε ἐν Χριστῷ Ἰησοῦ. 29 εἰ δὲ ὑμεῖς Χριστοῦ, ἄρα τοῦ Ἀβραὰμ σπέρμα ἐστέ, κατ' ἐπαγγελίαν κληρονόμοι.

4 Λέγω δέ, ἐφ' ὅσον χρόνον ὁ κληρονόμος νήπιός ἐστιν, οὐδὲν διαφέρει δούλου κύριος πάντων ὤν, 2 ἀλλὰ ὑπὸ ἐπιτρόπους ἐστὶν καὶ οἰκονόμους ἄχρι τῆς προθεσμίας τοῦ πατρός. 3 οὕτως καὶ ἡμεῖς, ὅτε ἦμεν νήπιοι, ὑπὸ τὰ στοιχεῖα τοῦ κόσμου ἤμεθα δεδουλωμένοι· 4 ὅτε δὲ ἦλθεν τὸ πλήρωμα τοῦ χρόνου, ἐξαπέστειλεν ὁ θεὸς τὸν υἱὸν αὐτοῦ, γενόμενον ἐκ γυναικός, γενόμενον ὑπὸ νόμον, 5 ἵνα τοὺς ὑπὸ νόμον ἐξαγοράσῃ, ἵνα τὴν υἱοθεσίαν ἀπολάβωμεν. 6 Ὅτι δέ ἐστε υἱοί, ἐξαπέστειλεν ὁ θεὸς τὸ πνεῦμα τοῦ υἱοῦ αὐτοῦ εἰς τὰς καρδίας ἡμῶν[1] κρᾶζον, Αββα ὁ πατήρ. 7 ὥστε οὐκέτι εἶ δοῦλος ἀλλὰ υἱός· εἰ δὲ υἱός, καὶ κληρονόμος διὰ θεοῦ[2].

---

[1] 6 {B} ἡμῶν p[46] ℵ A B C D* G P 104 1241 1739 1881 1962 1984 1985 l[597,598] it[ar,d,e,f,g,m,r3,x,z] vg[ww] syr[pal] cop[sa,boms] arm Marcion Tertullian Origen[lat] Ambrosiaster Hilary Athanasius Basil Jerome Augustine Cyril Euthalius Ps-Athanasius[gr,lat] ∥ ὑμῶν D[c] K L Ψ 33 81 88 181 326 330 436 451 614 629 630 1877 2127 2492 2495 Byz Lect it[dem] vg[cl] syr[p,h] cop[boms] goth eth Victorinus-Rome Ephraem Didymus Chrysostom Augustine Cyril Theodoret John-Damascus

[2] 7 {B} διὰ θεοῦ p[46] ℵ* A B C* 33 1739*[vid] it[dem,f,g,r3,x,z] vg cop[bo] Clement Ambrosiaster Victorinus-Rome Basil Ambrose Didymus[2/3] Augustine Cyril Primasius ∥ θεοῦ 1962 arm eth[ro] ∥ διὰ θεόν G[gr] 1881 ∥ διὰ Χριστοῦ 81 630 syr[pal] cop[sa] Jerome ∥ διὰ Ἰησοῦ Χριστοῦ 1739[c] l[55] (cop[boms]) ∥ θεοῦ διὰ Χριστοῦ ℵ[c] C[3] D K 88 104 181 330 436 451 614* 629 1241 1877 2492 Byz Lect it[ar,d,e] goth Didymus[1/3] Chrysostom Theodore[lat] Euthalius Theodoret John-Damascus ∥ θεοῦ διὰ Ἰησοῦ Χριστοῦ P 326 614[c] 2127 2495 syr[p,h] eth[pp] Theodoret ∥ διὰ θεοῦ ἐν Χριστῷ Ἰησοῦ cop[boms] ∥ μὲν θεοῦ συγκληρονόμος δὲ Χριστοῦ (see Ro 8.17) Ψ 1984 1985 Theodoret Theophylact

---

29 τοῦ Ἀβραάμ...κληρονόμοι Ro 4.13
4 3 ὑπὸ...δεδουλωμένοι Ga 3.23; Col 2.20 4 τὸ πλήρωμα τοῦ χρόνου Eph 1.10 τὸν υἱὸν ...γυναικός Jn 1.14; Ro 1.3 5 τοὺς...ἐξαγοράσῃ Ga 3.13 τὴν υἱοθεσίαν ἀπολάβωμεν Ro 8.15 6 Ro 8.15–16 7 εἰ δὲ...θεοῦ Ro 8.17; Ga 3.29

among you Jew or Greek, slave or freedman, male or female*—for you are all in fact one, in Christ Jesus.ᵃ **29** Further, if you belong to Christ you are thereby Abraham's offspring, inheritors of what was promised!ᵇ

■ CHAPTER FOUR ■

Christ Made Us Free Sons of God

1 I argue thus: as long as a designated heir is not of age, his condition is no different from that of a slave, though he is titular master of all his possessions; **2** for he is under the supervision of guardians and administrators until the time set by his father. **3** In the same way we also, while still not yet of age, were in a state of slavery, subordinated to the elemental powersᶜ* of the world. **4** But when the established time-limitᵈ* had been fulfilled, God sent forth his Son,* born of a womanᵉ and born into the framework of the Law— **5** expressly for the purpose of buying release from the Lawᶠ for those who were subject to it, so that we might receive* our status of adopted sons.ᵍ* **6** What proves that you are sons is the fact that God has sent forth into our* hearts the Spirit of his Son,* which cries out "Abba!", "Father!" **7** Therefore you are no longer a slave; you are a son! And by the very fact of being a son, you are also an heir,ʰ by God's doing.*

Paul's Concern for the Galatians

8 Ἀλλὰ τότε μὲν οὐκ εἰδότες θεὸν ἐδουλεύσατε τοῖς φύσει μὴ οὖσιν θεοῖς· 9 νῦν δὲ γνόντες θεόν, μᾶλλον δὲ γνωσθέντες ὑπὸ θεοῦ, πῶς ἐπιστρέφετε πάλιν ἐπὶ τὰ ἀσθενῆ καὶ πτωχὰ στοιχεῖα οἷς πάλιν ἄνωθεν δουλεύειν θέλετε; 10 ἡμέρας παρατηρεῖσθε καὶ μῆνας καὶ καιροὺς καὶ ἐνιαυτούς,[a] 11 φοβοῦμαι ὑμᾶς μή πως εἰκῇ κεκοπίακα εἰς ὑμᾶς.
12 Γίνεσθε ὡς ἐγώ, ὅτι κἀγὼ ὡς ὑμεῖς, ἀδελφοί, δέομαι ὑμῶν. οὐδέν με ἠδικήσατε· 13 οἴδατε δὲ ὅτι δι' ἀσθένειαν τῆς σαρκὸς εὐηγγελισάμην ὑμῖν τὸ πρότερον, 14 καὶ τὸν πειρασμὸν ὑμῶν[3] ἐν τῇ σαρκί μου οὐκ ἐξουθενήσατε οὐδὲ ἐξεπτύσατε, ἀλλὰ ὡς ἄγγελον θεοῦ ἐδέξασθέ με, ὡς Χριστὸν Ἰησοῦν. 15 ποῦ οὖν ὁ μακαρισμὸς ὑμῶν; μαρτυρῶ γὰρ ὑμῖν ὅτι εἰ δυνατὸν τοὺς ὀφθαλμοὺς ὑμῶν ἐξορύξαντες ἐδώκατέ μοι. 16 ὥστε ἐχθρὸς ὑμῶν γέγονα ἀληθεύων ὑμῖν; 17 ζηλοῦσιν ὑμᾶς οὐ καλῶς, ἀλλὰ ἐκκλεῖσαι ὑμᾶς θέλουσιν, ἵνα αὐτοὺς ζηλοῦτε· 18 καλὸν δὲ ζηλοῦσθαι ἐν καλῷ πάντοτε καὶ μὴ μόνον ἐν τῷ παρεῖναί με πρὸς ὑμᾶς.[b] 19 τέκνα μου, οὓς πάλιν ὠδίνω μέχρις οὗ μορφωθῇ Χριστὸς ἐν ὑμῖν·[b] 20 ἤθελον δὲ παρεῖναι πρὸς ὑμᾶς ἄρτι καὶ ἀλλάξαι τὴν φωνήν μου, ὅτι ἀποροῦμαι ἐν ὑμῖν.

---

[3] 14 {B} τὸν πειρασμὸν ὑμῶν ℵ* A B C² D* G 33 it[d,dem,e,f,g,r³,z] vg cop[bo] Ambrosiaster Victorinus-Rome Jerome Augustine ∥ τὸν πειρασμὸν ὑμῶν τόν 1739 1881 (Origen) ∥ τὸν πειρασμόν μου p[46] it[ar,x] ∥ τὸν πειρασμόν μου τόν C*[vid] D[(b),c] K P Ψ 181 330 451 614 629 630 1877 1962 2127 2492 2495 Byz Lect syr[h] cop[sa,boms] Chrysostom Cyril Theodoret John-Damascus ∥ τὸν πειρασμὸν τόν ℵ[c] 81 88 104 326 436 1241 1984 1985 syr[p] goth arm eth Basil Euthalius Theophylact

[a] 10 a statement: TR WH Bov BF² AV RV ASV NEB Zür Luth ∥ a exclamation: RSV Jer Seg ∥ a question

[bb] 18–19 b major, b major: NEB ∥ b minor, b major: TR WH Bov BF² Zür Jer ∥ b minor, b exclamation: Luth ∥ b major, b minor: AV RV Seg ∥ b major, b exclamation: RSV ∥ b major, b dash: ASV

8 τοῖς...θεοῖς 2 Chr 13.9; Is 37.19; Jr 2.11; 1 Cor 8.4–6   13 δι'...ὑμῖν 1 Cor 2.3   16 Am 5.10

Do Not Throw This Freedom Away!

8 Of course formerly, not knowing God, you served as slaves to gods who are not really divine.ª* **9** But now that you have come to know God—or rather, have been recognized by him*—how can you turn back again to those weak and beggarly* elemental powers? Are you willing to enslave yourselves to them all over again? **10** Are you actually keeping ceremonial observance of days, months, seasons, years?ᵇ* **11** You fill me with fear that I have wasted my efforts on you!

The Galatians' Former Enthusiasm and Devotion

12 My brethren, I implore you to be as I am,* since I am also like you. (You have done me no harm!) **13** You remember that it was a bodily ailmentᶜ that originally occasioned my bringing you the Gospel.* **14** My physical condition was a challenge which you did not despise or brush aside in disgust;* rather you took me to yourselves as if an angel from God, as if Christ Jesus! **15** So where is that grateful joy of yours now? Indeed, I can testify to your credit that if it had been possible you would have plucked out your eyes and given them to me! **16** Have I therefor become your hated enemy because I speak out to you the truth?ᵈ* **17** Those people are not courting your favor with honorable intentions!ᵉ What they really want is to lock you out, and make you envy them.* **18** It is of course always an honor to be courted honorably—and not only when I am among you.* **19** My children, I am once more in the pangs of childbirth with you until Christ takes form in you!ᶠ **20** If only I could be with you now, and could adapt my tone! Really, I am in a quandary over you!

The Allegory of Hagar and Sarah

21 Λέγετέ μοι, οἱ ὑπὸ νόμον θέλοντες εἶναι, τὸν νόμον οὐκ ἀκούετε; 22 γέγραπται γὰρ ὅτι Ἀβραὰμ δύο υἱοὺς ἔσχεν, ἕνα ἐκ τῆς παιδίσκης καὶ ἕνα ἐκ τῆς ἐλευθέρας. 23 ἀλλ' ὁ μὲν ἐκ τῆς παιδίσκης κατὰ σάρκα γεγέννηται, ὁ δὲ ἐκ τῆς ἐλευθέρας δι' ἐπαγγελίας. 24 ἅτινά ἐστιν ἀλληγορούμενα· αὗται γάρ εἰσιν δύο διαθῆκαι, μία μὲν ἀπὸ ὄρους Σινᾶ εἰς δουλείαν γεννῶσα, ἥτις ἐστὶν Ἀγάρ. 25 τὸ δὲ Ἀγὰρ Σινᾶ[4] ὄρος ἐστὶν ἐν τῇ Ἀραβίᾳ· συστοιχεῖ δὲ τῇ νῦν Ἰερουσαλήμ, δουλεύει γὰρ μετὰ τῶν τέκνων αὐτῆς. 26 ἡ δὲ ἄνω Ἰερουσαλὴμ ἐλευθέρα ἐστίν, ἥτις ἐστὶν μήτηρ ἡμῶν·[5] 27 γέγραπται γάρ,

Εὐφράνθητι, στεῖρα ἡ οὐ τίκτουσα,
ῥῆξον καὶ βόησον, ἡ οὐκ ὠδίνουσα·
ὅτι πολλὰ τὰ τέκνα τῆς ἐρήμου μᾶλλον ἢ τῆς ἐχούσης τὸν ἄνδρα.

28 ὑμεῖς[6] δέ, ἀδελφοί, κατὰ Ἰσαὰκ ἐπαγγελίας τέκνα

---

[4] 25 {D} δὲ Ἀγὰρ Σινᾶ A B D^gr 88 330 436 451 1962 2127 2492 Lect syr^hmg,pal cop^bo ∥ γὰρ Ἀγὰρ Σινᾶ K P Ψ 062 33 81 104 181 326 614 629 630 1877 1881 1984^c 1985 2495 Byz l^1364,1365 syr^p,h cop^bomss arm Chrysostom Theodore^lat Cyril Theodoret Ps-Oecumenius Theophylact ∥ δὲ Σινᾶ p^46 it^t,x,z cop^sa Ambrosiaster ∥ γὰρ Ἀγάρ it^d,e (Ambrosiaster^coinm) ∥ γὰρ Σινᾶ ℵ C G 1241 1739 1984* it^ar,f,g,r3 vg eth Origen^lat Ambrosiaster^txt Victorinus-Rome Epiphanius Jerome Augustine Cyril John-Damascus ∥ Σινᾶ goth Augustine

[5] 26 {B} ἡμῶν p^46 ℵ* B C* D G Ψ 33 88 1241 1739 1881 2495 it^d,dem, e,f,g,r3,x,z vg syr^p,hmg cop^sa,bo goth eth Marcion Irenaeus Tertullian Origen Pamphilus Eusebius Ambrosiaster Hilary Ephraem Gregory-Elvira Chrysostom Jerome Augustine Marcus Isidore Cyril Theodoret ∥ πάντων ἡμῶν ℵ^c A C^3 K P 81 104 181 326 330 436 451 614 629 630 1877 1962 1984 1985 2127 2492 Byz Lect it^ar,t syr^h,pal arm Irenaeus^lat Origen^lat Eusebius Victorinus-Rome Hilary Cyril-Jerusalem Ambrose Macarius Pelagius Jerome Theodore^lat Augustine Euthalius Theodoret Cosmas Cassiodorus John-Damascus

[6] 28 {B} ὑμεῖς...ἐστέ. p^46 B D* G 33 1739 1881 2127 it^d,e,g,t syr^pal cop^sa

---

22 ἕνα ἐκ τῆς παιδίσκης Gn 16.15   ἕνα ἐκ τῆς ἐλευθέρας Gn 21.2   23 Ro 9.7-9
24 μία...γεννῶσα Ro 8.15; Ga 5.1   26 ἡ δὲ ἄνω Ἰερουσαλήμ He 12.22; Re 3.12; 21.2, 10
27 Εὐφράνθητι...ἄνδρα Is 54.1   28 κατὰ...ἐστέ Ro 9.7; Ga 3.29

An Allegory Illustrating Christian Freedom

21 Tell me, you who want to be subject to the Law, do you not hear what the Law says? 22 It is written, remember, that Abraham had two sons, one from the slave-girl,ᵃ the other from his free-born wife.ᵇ 23 The difference was that the son of the slave-girl had been begotten by natural procreation,⋆ but the son of the free woman was the fruit of the Promise.ᶜ 24 All this is clearly an allegory: the two women stand for the two covenants; one covenant⋆ was from Mount Sinai, bringing forth children into slavery; this is Hagar. 25 Now Hagar is Sinai,⋆ a mountain in Arabia, but corresponds⋆ to the Jerusalem of our time, for she and her children are in slavery.ᵈ⋆ 26 But the Jerusalem on highᵉ is free-born, and it is she who is our mother!⋆ 27 That is why Scripture says:

Rejoice, you barren one who have brought forth no children; break forth in jubilant song you who have not known the pangs of birth! For many are the children of the deserted wife—more than of her who has a husband!⋆

28 Now you,⋆ my brethren, are children of the Promise, in the manner of Isaac.ᶠ

ἐστέ.⁶ 29 ἀλλ' ὥσπερ τότε ὁ κατὰ σάρκα γεννηθεὶς ἐδίωκεν τὸν κατὰ πνεῦμα, οὕτως καὶ νῦν. 30 ἀλλὰ τί λέγει ἡ γραφή; **Ἔκβαλε τὴν παιδίσκην καὶ τὸν υἱὸν αὐτῆς· οὐ γὰρ μὴ κληρονομήσει ὁ υἱὸς τῆς παιδίσκης μετὰ τοῦ υἱοῦ** τῆς ἐλευθέρας. 31 διό, ἀδελφοί, οὐκ ἐσμὲν παιδίσκης τέκνα ἀλλὰ τῆς ἐλευθέρας. **5** τῇ ἐλευθερίᾳ ἡμᾶς Χριστὸς ἠλευθέρωσεν· στήκετε οὖν[1] καὶ μὴ πάλιν ζυγῷ δουλείας ἐνέχεσθε.

Christian Freedom

2 **Ἴδε ἐγὼ Παῦλος λέγω ὑμῖν ὅτι ἐὰν περιτέμνησθε, Χριστὸς ὑμᾶς οὐδὲν ὠφελήσει.** 3 μαρτύρομαι δὲ πάλιν παντὶ ἀνθρώπῳ περιτεμνομένῳ ὅτι ὀφειλέτης ἐστὶν ὅλον τὸν νόμον ποιῆσαι. 4 **κατηργήθητε ἀπὸ Χριστοῦ, οἵτινες**

eth[ro] Irenaeus[gr,lat] Origen[acc. to Jerome] Ambrosiaster Victorinus-Rome Tyconius Ambrose ∥ ἡμεῖς...ἐσμέν. ℵ A C D[c] K P Ψ 062 81 88 104 181 326 330 436 451 614 629 630 1241 1877 1962 1984 1985 2492 2495 *Byz Lect* it[ar,dem, f,r3,x,z] vg syr[p,h] cop[bo] goth arm eth[pp] Chrysostom Jerome Augustine Cyril Euthalius Theodoret John-Damascus

[1] **1** {C} τῇ ἐλευθερίᾳ ἡμᾶς Χριστὸς ἠλευθέρωσεν· στήκετε οὖν ℵ* A B (P εἱλευθέρωσεν) 33 (2127 *omit* ἡμᾶς *and read* στῆτε) syr[pal] cop[sa] (cop[bo] τῇ γάρ) ∥ τῇ ἐλευθερίᾳ Χριστὸς ἡμᾶς ἠλευθέρωσεν· στήκετε οὖν ℵ[c] (C* ἐλευθέρωσεν) (C² add οὖν *after* ἐλευθερίᾳ) (H 1962 στῆτε οὖν) Ψ 81 (104 *add* ᾗ *after* ἐλευθερίᾳ) (181[c] *omit* οὖν) 330 451 1241 1739 1881 2492 (*l*598) ∥ τῇ ἐλευθερίᾳ ἡμᾶς Χριστὸς ἠλευθέρωσεν· στήκετε D[gr*] (D[b] ᾗ Χριστὸς ἡμᾶς, D[c] ἡμᾶς ᾗ Χριστός) (614 *add* οὖν *after* ἐλευθερίᾳ) (it[ar,x]) ∥ τῇ ἐλευθερίᾳ οὖν ᾗ Χριστὸς ἡμᾶς ἠλευθέρωσεν στήκετε, K 88 181* (326 *add* οὖν) (436 ὁ *for* ᾗ) 629 (630 ὑμᾶς) (1984 ὁ Χριστὸς ἠλευθέρωσεν ἡμᾶς) (1985 ἠλευθέρωσεν ἡμᾶς) *Byz Lect* (*l*603,809 *omit* ᾗ) ∥ τῇ ἐλευθερίᾳ ᾗ ὁ Χριστὸς ἡμᾶς ἐξηγόρασε, στήκετε 2495 ∥ ᾗ ἐλευθερίᾳ ἡμᾶς Χριστὸς ἠλευθέρωσεν, στήκετε οὖν G (1877 *transposes*: ἐλευθερίᾳ οὖν Χριστὸς ἡμᾶς) it[f,g,r3] (syr[p,h]) goth (arm Χριστὸς ἡμᾶς) Ambrosiaster ∥ ᾗ ἐλευθερίᾳ ἡμᾶς Χριστὸς ἠλευθέρωσεν, στήκετε it[d,e] vg[ww] (it[dem] vg[cl] eth Χριστὸς ἡμᾶς)

29 ὁ κατὰ...πνεῦμα Gn 21.9   **30** Ἔκβαλε...υἱοῦ Gn 21.10; (Jn 8.35)   **31** Ga 3.29
5 1 τῇ...ἠλευθέρωσεν Jn 8.32, 36; Ga 2.4; 5.13   ζυγῷ δουλείας ἐνέχεσθε Ac 15.10

29 But just as in those days the son born according to the flesh persecuted* the one born according to the spirit, it is the very same now. 30 But what does Scripture say? *Cast out the slave-girl with her son; for the son of the slave-girl shall never be heir with the son** of the woman born free. 31 Therefore, my brethren, we are children not of a slave-girl but of a mother who is free.ª

■ CHAPTER FIVE ■

IV. EXHORTATION TO CHRISTIAN LIVING

The Basic Importance of Faith

1 It was for a life of freedom that Christ freed us;ᵇ* so* stand firm and do not entangle yourselves again with the yoke of slavery!ᶜ 2 Pay attention: I, Paul, am telling you that if ever you have yourselves circumcised, Christ will be of no benefit to you at all!ᵈ 3 Once more I solemnly point out to every person who receives circumcision that he is obligated to carry out the Law in its entirety. 4 Any of you who put your justification in the Law have divorced yourselves* from Christ and fallen out of God's favor!

ἐν νόμῳ δικαιοῦσθε, τῆς χάριτος ἐξεπέσατε. 5 ἡμεῖς γὰρ πνεύματι ἐκ πίστεως ἐλπίδα δικαιοσύνης ἀπεκδεχόμεθα. 6 ἐν γὰρ Χριστῷ Ἰησοῦ οὔτε περιτομή τι ἰσχύει οὔτε ἀκροβυστία ἀλλὰ πίστις δι' ἀγάπης ἐνεργουμένη. 7 Ἐτρέχετε καλῶς· τίς ὑμᾶς ἐνέκοψεν [τῇ] ἀληθείᾳ μὴ πείθεσθαι; 8 ἡ πεισμονὴ οὐκ ἐκ τοῦ καλοῦντος ὑμᾶς. 9 μικρὰ ζύμη ὅλον τὸ φύραμα ζυμοῖ. 10 ἐγὼ πέποιθα εἰς ὑμᾶς ἐν κυρίῳ ὅτι οὐδὲν ἄλλο φρονήσετε· ὁ δὲ ταράσσων ὑμᾶς βαστάσει τὸ κρίμα, ὅστις ἐὰν ᾖ. 11 ἐγὼ δέ, ἀδελφοί, εἰ περιτομὴν ἔτι κηρύσσω, τί ἔτι διώκομαι; ἄρα κατήργηται τὸ σκάνδαλον τοῦ σταυροῦ. 12 ὄφελον καὶ ἀποκόψονται οἱ ἀναστατοῦντες ὑμᾶς.

13 Ὑμεῖς γὰρ ἐπ' ἐλευθερίᾳ ἐκλήθητε, ἀδελφοί· μόνον μὴ τὴν ἐλευθερίαν εἰς ἀφορμὴν τῇ σαρκί, ἀλλὰ διὰ τῆς ἀγάπης δουλεύετε ἀλλήλοις. 14 ὁ γὰρ πᾶς νόμος ἐν ἑνὶ λόγῳ πεπλήρωται, ἐν τῷ **Ἀγαπήσεις τὸν πλησίον σου ὡς σεαυτόν**. 15 εἰ δὲ ἀλλήλους δάκνετε καὶ κατεσθίετε, βλέπετε μὴ ὑπ' ἀλλήλων ἀναλωθῆτε.

The Fruit of the Spirit and the Works of the Flesh

16 Λέγω δέ, πνεύματι περιπατεῖτε καὶ ἐπιθυμίαν σαρκὸς οὐ μὴ τελέσητε. 17 ἡ γὰρ σὰρξ ἐπιθυμεῖ κατὰ τοῦ πνεύματος, τὸ δὲ πνεῦμα κατὰ τῆς σαρκός, ταῦτα γὰρ ἀλλήλοις ἀντίκειται, ἵνα μὴ ἃ ἐὰν θέλητε ταῦτα ποιῆτε. 18 εἰ δὲ πνεύματι ἄγεσθε, οὐκ ἐστὲ ὑπὸ νόμον. 19 φανερὰ δέ ἐστιν τὰ ἔργα τῆς σαρκός, ἅτινά ἐστιν πορνεία, ἀκαθαρσία, ἀσέλγεια, 20 εἰδωλολατρία, φαρμακεία, ἔχθραι, ἔρις, ζῆλος, θυμοί, ἐριθεῖαι, διχοστασίαι, αἱρέσεις, 21 φθόνοι[2], μέθαι, κῶμοι καὶ τὰ ὅμοια τού-

---

[2] 21 {D} φθόνοι p^{46} ℵ B 33 81 2492 $l^{603,809}$ it^t cop^{sa} Marcion Irenaeus^{lat} Clement Origen^{lat} Ambrosiaster Epiphanius Chrysostom$^{1/2}$ Jerome Augus-

---

6 οὔτε περιτομή...ἀκροβυστία 1 Cor 7.19; Ga 6.15   8 τοῦ καλοῦντος ὑμᾶς Ga 1.6
9 1 Cor 5.6   11 τὸ σκάνδαλον τοῦ σταυροῦ 1 Cor 1.23   13 μόνον...σαρκί 1 Pe 2.16
14 Ἀγαπήσεις...σεαυτόν Lv 19.18 (Mt 5.43; 19.19; 22.39; Mk 12.31; Lk 10.27; Ro 13.9; Jas 2.8)
16 πνεύματι περιπατεῖτε Ro 8.4; Ga 5.25   17 Ro 7.15-23   ἡ γὰρ...ἀντίκειται 1 Pe 2.11
18 πνεύματι ἄγεσθε Ro 8.14   οὐκ...νόμον Ro 6.14; 7.4   19–21 1 Cor 6.9–10; Eph 5.5; Re 22.15

5 For we★ are eagerly awaiting on the spiritual level our hoped-for justification, a fruit of faith. 6 For in Christ Jesus, neither circumcision nor its absence means anything[a]★—only faith expressing itself through love.★

Be Not Misled!

7 You were running along well;★ who has hindered you from following the truth? 8 That enticement does not come from him★ who called you![b] 9 A little yeast ferments the whole batch of dough.[c] 10 I have put my trust in you in the Lord, that you will not take up other opinions.★ But he who is unsettling you will bear the condemnation, whoever he may be. 11 As for me, my brethren, if I am even now continuing to advocate circumcision,★ why am I still being attacked? In that case, the cross has ceased to be a stumbling-block![d]★ 12 If only those who are upsetting you would end up castrating themselves!★

Our Liberty Should Be Used for Good Conduct

13 My brethren, remember that you have been called to live in freedom—only not a freedom which gives free rein★ to the flesh.[e] Rather, in your mutual love put yourselves at one another's service.★ 14 For the whole Law has found its fulfillment in this one phrase: *You shall love your neighbor as yourself.*[f]★ 15 If instead you go on biting and devouring one another, look out or you will consume each other!

16 My point is: live in accord with the spirit;[g] then you will not carry out the cravings of the flesh. 17 For the flesh hungers against the spirit, and the spirit against the flesh; these two are directly opposed to one another.[h] That is why you do not carry out whatever★ your will intends. 18 But if you let yourselves be guided by the Spirit,[i] you are not under any law.[j] 19 Now it is obvious what proceeds from the flesh —lewd conduct, impurity, licentiousness, 20 idolatry, sorcery, hatreds, contentiousness, jealousy, outbursts of rage, selfish rivalries, dissensions, factions, 21 feeling of envy,★ drunkenness, orgies of debauchery, and the like.[k] I warn you,

τοις, ἃ προλέγω ὑμῖν, καθὼς προεῖπον ὅτι οἱ τὰ τοιαῦτα πράσσοντες βασιλείαν θεοῦ οὐ κληρονομήσουσιν.

22 Ὁ δὲ καρπὸς τοῦ πνεύματός ἐστιν ἀγάπη χαρὰ εἰρήνη, μακροθυμία χρηστότης ἀγαθωσύνη, πίστις 23ᵃ πραΰτης ἐγκράτεια· ᵃκατὰ τῶν τοιούτων οὐκ ἔστιν νόμος. 24 οἱ δὲ τοῦ Χριστοῦ [Ἰησοῦ] τὴν σάρκα ἐσταύρωσαν σὺν τοῖς παθήμασιν καὶ ταῖς ἐπιθυμίαις. 25 εἰ ζῶμεν πνεύματι, πνεύματι καὶ στοιχῶμεν. 26 μὴ γινώμεθα κενόδοξοι, ἀλλήλους προκαλούμενοι, ἀλλήλοις φθονοῦντες.

Bear One Another's Burdens

6 Ἀδελφοί, ἐὰν καὶ προλημφθῇ ἄνθρωπος ἔν τινι παραπτώματι, ὑμεῖς οἱ πνευματικοὶ καταρτίζετε τὸν τοιοῦτον ἐν πνεύματι πραΰτητος, σκοπῶν σεαυτὸν μὴ καὶ σὺ πειρασθῇς. 2 Ἀλλήλων τὰ βάρη βαστάζετε καὶ οὕτως ἀναπληρώσετε¹ τὸν νόμον τοῦ Χριστοῦ. 3 εἰ γὰρ δοκεῖ τις εἶναί τι μηδὲν ὤν, φρεναπατᾷ ἑαυτόν. 4 τὸ δὲ ἔργον ἑαυτοῦ δοκιμαζέτω ἕκαστος, καὶ τότε εἰς ἑαυτὸν

---

tine Euthalius ∥ φθόνοι φόνοι A C D G K P Ψ 0122 88 104 181 326 330 436 451 (629 *transposes*: φθόνοι αἱρέσεις φόνοι) 630 1241 1739 1877 1881 1962 1985 2127 2495 *Byz Lect* it^(ar,c,d,(dem),e,f,g,x,z) vg syr^(p,h) cop^(bo) goth arm eth (Cyprian) Ambrosiaster Lucifer Ephraem Priscillian Chrysostom^(1/2) Latin mss^(acc. to Jerome) Theodore^(lat) Theodoret John-Damascus

¹ 2 {C} ἀναπληρώσετε B G 1962 it^(ar,d,dem,e,f,g,t,x,z) vg syr^(p,pal) cop^(sa,bo) goth eth Marcion Tertullian Cyprian Asterius^(acc. to Photius) Ambrosiaster Victorinus-Rome Basil^(1/2) Orosius Jerome Augustine Marcus Proclus Theodoret ∥ ἀποπληρώσετε p⁴⁶ ∥ ἀναπληρώσατε ℵ A C D^(gr) K P Ψ 0122 33 81 88 104 181 326 330 436 451 614 629 630 1241 1739 1877 1881 1985 2127 2492 2495 *Byz Lect* syr^h arm Clement Ephraem Athanasius Basil^(1/2) Didymus Chrysostom Euthalius Theodoret John-Damascus

---

ᵃ ᵃ 22-23 *a number 23, a no number*: TR^(ed) WH Bov BF² AV RV ASV RSV NEB? Zür Jer Seg ∥ *a no number, a number 23*: TR^(ed) NEB? Luth

22 Ὁ δὲ...πνεύματος Eph 5.9   23 κατὰ...νόμος 1 Tm 1.9   24 Ro 6.6; Col 3.5
25 πνεύματι καὶ στοιχῶμεν Ro 8.4; Ga 5.16   26 μὴ γινώμεθα κενόδοξοι Php 2.3
6 1 ἐὰν...τοιοῦτον Mt 18.15; Jas 5.19   2 Ἀλλήλων...βαστάζετε Ro 15.1   4 τὸ δὲ...ἕκαστος 1 Cor 11.28; 2 Cor 13.5

as I have warned you before: those who do such things will not inherit the kingdom of God!

22 In contrast, the fruit of the Spirit is love, joy, peace, patient endurance, kindness, generosity, faith, 23 mildness, self-control.ᵃ Against such there is no law!ᵇ★ 24 Now those who belong to Christ [Jesus] have crucified their flesh with its passions and desires.ᶜ 25 If we live by the Spirit, let us in fact follow the Spirit's lead.ᵈ 26 Let us never be boastful,ᵉ a source of provocation to others, or jealous of one another.

■ CHAPTER SIX ■

Let Each Look to His Own Conscience

1 My brethren, even if a person be found surprised into some sin,★ you who are spiritual should set him right in a spirit of gentleness, each of you looking to yourself to avoid also falling into temptation.ᶠ 2 Help carry one another's burdens,★ and in that way fulfill★ the law of Christ. 3 Surely if anyone thinks he is something, when he is really nothing, he is deluding himself.ᵍ 4 Each one should examine his own

μόνον τὸ καύχημα ἕξει καὶ οὐκ εἰς τὸν ἕτερον· 5 ἕκαστος γὰρ τὸ ἴδιον φορτίον βαστάσει. 6 Κοινωνείτω δὲ ὁ κατηχούμενος τὸν λόγον τῷ κατηχοῦντι ἐν πᾶσιν ἀγαθοῖς. 7 Μὴ πλανᾶσθε, θεὸς οὐ μυκτηρίζεται. ὃ γὰρ ἐὰν σπείρῃ ἄνθρωπος, τοῦτο καὶ θερίσει· 8 ὅτι ὁ σπείρων εἰς τὴν σάρκα ἑαυτοῦ ἐκ τῆς σαρκὸς θερίσει φθοράν, ὁ δὲ σπείρων εἰς τὸ πνεῦμα ἐκ τοῦ πνεύματος θερίσει ζωὴν αἰώνιον. 9 τὸ δὲ καλὸν ποιοῦντες μὴ ἐγκακῶμεν, καιρῷ γὰρ ἰδίῳ θερίσομεν μὴ ἐκλυόμενοι. 10 ἄρα οὖν ὡς καιρὸν ἔχομεν, ἐργαζώμεθα τὸ ἀγαθὸν πρὸς πάντας, μάλιστα δὲ πρὸς τοὺς οἰκείους τῆς πίστεως.

Final Warning and Benediction

11 Ἴδετε πηλίκοις ὑμῖν γράμμασιν ἔγραψα τῇ ἐμῇ χειρί. 12 ὅσοι θέλουσιν εὐπροσωπῆσαι ἐν σαρκί, οὗτοι ἀναγκάζουσιν ὑμᾶς περιτέμνεσθαι, μόνον ἵνα ᵃ τῷ σταυρῷ τοῦ Χριστοῦᵃ μὴ διώκωνται. 13 οὐδὲ γὰρ οἱ περιτεμνόμενοι² αὐτοὶ νόμον φυλάσσουσιν ἀλλὰ θέλουσιν ὑμᾶς περιτέμνεσθαι, ἵνα ἐν τῇ ὑμετέρᾳ σαρκὶ καυχήσωνται. 14 ἐμοὶ δὲ μὴ γένοιτο καυχᾶσθαι εἰ μὴ ἐν τῷ σταυρῷ τοῦ κυρίου ἡμῶν Ἰησοῦ Χριστοῦ, δι' οὗ ἐμοὶ κόσμος ἐσταύρωται κἀγὼ κόσμῳ. 15 οὔτε γὰρ περιτομή τί ἐστιν οὔτε ἀκροβυστία ἀλλὰ καινὴ κτίσις. 16 καὶ ὅσοι τῷ κανόνι τούτῳ στοιχήσουσιν, εἰρήνη ἐπ' αὐτοὺς καὶ ἔλεος καὶ ἐπὶ τὸν Ἰσραὴλ τοῦ θεοῦ.

² 13 {C} περιτεμνόμενοι ℵ A C D^gr K P 33 81 88 104 181 326 436 629 1241 1739 1877 1962 1984 1985 *Byz*^pt it^(ar,dem,f,x,z) vg syr^(p,h) arm Marcion Chrysostom Jerome Euthalius Theodoret John-Damascus ∥ περιτετμημένοι p^46 B (G περιτεμνημένοι) Ψ 330 451 614 630 2127 2492 2495 *Byz*^pt *Lect* it^(d,e,g,r3) cop^(sa,bo) goth eth Ambrosiaster Victorinus-Rome Pelagius Jerome Augustine

ᵃ ᵃ 12 *a a* no dashes: TR Bov BF² AV RV ASV RSV NEB Luth Jer Seg ∥ *a* none, *a* dash: WH ∥ *a* dash, *a* dash: Zür

5 Ro 14.12 6 1 Cor 9.11, 14 8 Jn 3.6; 6.63; Ro 8.13 9 τὸ δὲ...ἐγκακῶμεν 2 Th 3.13
12 οὗτοι...διώκωνται Ga 5.11 14 ἐμοὶ...Χριστοῦ 1 Cor 1.31; 2.2 15 οὔτε γὰρ... ἀκροβυστία 1 Cor 7.19; Ga 5.6 καινὴ κτίσις 2 Cor 5.17 16 εἰρήνη...Ἰσραὴλ Ps 125.5; 128.6

Explanatory Notes

1.1: Paul means he did not receive his authority from any church group or through any individual apostle as delegate, but was appointed directly by Christ as his emissary authorized to teach and act in Christ's name.

1.2: "brethren" (adelphoi) includes all fellow-believers in Christ, male or female.

1.4: The redemption was a 'rescue operation' from a world prostrate under the power of Satan. Cp. 2 Cor 4.4; Eph 2.2; 6.12.

1.6: "deserting": the word here (metatithesthe) has political overtones, used of changing parties.

1.6: "called you": many MSS read "called you in the grace of (Jesus) Christ."

1.7: There is only one faith, one baptism (Eph 4.3-6).

1.8: "curses": Literally, "Let him be anathema!"—an object of cursing. Paul is not merely venting his anger; he is using his apostolic authority to uphold Christ's truth.

1.10: Obviously repudiating a calumny which he knows has been used against him.

1.10: "approval": Before his conversion, Paul sought to win the esteem of his fellow Jews by fervent observance of the Law of Moses (cp.1.14 and Phil 3.6).

1.12: The Greek can also mean "because Jesus Christ was revealed to me."

1.15: Many MSS specify who "He" was, by adding "God."

1.15: "called me": this echoes Jer 1.5: "Before I formed you in the womb I knew you; before you were born I dedicated you, I appointed you a prophet to the nations."

1.16: "within me": this refers to Paul's profound conversion experience near Damascus (Acts 9.3-9)—which was much more than mere intellectual knowledge.

1.16: "human advisers": literally, "flesh and blood."

---

conduct,ᵃ★ and then if he has reason to boast of anything, it will be in relation to himself, not someone else. 5 In that way, each will bear his own load.ᵇ★

6 He who is instructed in the Word should share with his instructor all his goods.ᶜ★ 7 Make no mistake about it: no one outwits God!★ A man will reap only what he sows.ᵈ 8 If he sows in the field of the flesh, he will reap from it a harvest of corruption. But if his seed-ground is the spirit, from the spirit he will reap everlasting life.ᵉ 9 Let us not grow weary of doing good,ᶠ for if we do not relax our efforts, in due time we shall reap our harvest. 10 So while we have the opportunity,★ let us do good to all men,ᵍ but especially to those who are our kindred in the faith.

V. CONCLUSION

A Final Plea to Follow Christ

11 See with what bold script★ I have written to you, with my own hand!ʰ 12 It is persons who are seeking to make a good showing in the flesh★ who are pressuring you to be circumcised—and it is only that they may escape being persecuted on account of Christ's cross.ⁱ★ 13 Why, not even the very ones who accept★ circumcision follow out the Law themselves; they only want you to be circumcised so that they may boast over your bodily observance.

14 May I at least never boast except in the cross of our Lord Jesus Christ!ʲ Through it★ the world has been crucified to me, and I to the world.★ 15 Really, it means nothing whether one is circumcised or not;ᵏ *what does count is that one be created anew.*ˡ 16 Peace and mercy upon all who follow this principle; that is upon the Israel of God.ᵐ

17 Τοῦ λοιποῦ κόπους μοι μηδεὶς παρεχέτω· ἐγὼ γὰρ τὰ στίγματα τοῦ Ἰησοῦ ἐν τῷ σώματί μου βαστάζω.

18 Ἡ χάρις τοῦ κυρίου ἡμῶν Ἰησοῦ Χριστοῦ μετὰ τοῦ πνεύματος ὑμῶν, ἀδελφοί· ἀμήν.

---

17 ἐγώ...βαστάζω 2 Cor 4.10

17 From now on, let no man bother me! See, I b[ear in] my body the brand-marks of my belonging to Jesus![a]

18 Brethren, may the favor of our Lord Jesus Chr[ist be] with your spirit! Amen.

GALATIANS 73

1.17: "Arabia": probably the region of the Nabataean Arabs, east and south of Damascus and the Dead Sea, including Petra.

1.18: Kephas was the Aramaic name of Simon (Peter); cp. Mt 16.16-18. Paul implies that he questioned Peter on Christ's teaching and actions.

1.19: This James was not one of the twelve apostles, but an important witness to the life and teaching of Jesus. He became the first leader of the Church of Jerusalem. Paul's word here, "brother," is a loose term for "relative"—for instance, the Roman Emperor Marcus Aurelius calls his brother-in-law Severus "my brother" (Med. 1.14). Similar usage at Gn 13.8; 14.14; 29.12; Lv 10.4, etc.

1.21: "Cilicia": including Tarsus, where Paul was born and grew up.

2.1: This 'Council of Jerusalem' is described at Acts 15.1-35.

2.1: Titus was one of Paul's faithful companions in promoting the Gospel. Cp.2 Cor 2.13; 7.6, 13-15; 8.6,16,23; 12.18. Paul left him in charge of the church in Crete, and wrote him fatherly instructions in 1 and 2 Titus.

2.2: "revelation": Paul wants it known that he had not been summoned to Jerusalem by the apostles to be investigated.

2.2: "leaders": *hoi dokountes*, literally "those held in repute," "those who seemed to be important."

2.4: "It": the whole discussion of Paul's policy of not requiring pagan converts to take on the obligations of the Mosaic Law.

2.5: Acts 15.7-11 credits Peter also for supporting Gentile converts.

2.6: "favorites": that is, God does not regard a person's external circumstances or appearance in place of one's real worth. Paul's image is from the theater: *prosopon* means "mask" and "role played."

2.6: Perhaps an echo of Dt 5.6-21, where Moses says that God, after giving the Ten Commandments, "added no more."

2.7: Literally, "the uncircumcised" (pagans) and "the circumcised" (Jews). It is possible to translate this passage as "I was entrusted with the Gospel of uncircumcision, just as Peter was that of circumcision." This refers only to their primary emphasis, as Paul also sought to convert Jews, and Peter Gentiles.2.11: For this meaning of *kata prosopon* cp. 2 Cor 10.1 and Acts 25.16.

2.11: "self-condemned": A legal term in judgments, *kategnosmenos* here is likely middle voice **(self-condemned),** not passive **(condemned by others).** Peter's actions in going along with the Judaizers for the sake of peace did not square with his own known convictions that Christians need not observe the whole Law of Moses. His example threatened to promote opposed factions within the Church and destroy the unity of a common Eucharistic meal. Cp. Rom 14.23: "If someone eats while his conscience has misgivings about it, he condemns himself, for he is not acting according to his belief."

2.12: "Gentiles": sc. converts from paganism; the "circumcised" are converted Jews.

2.12: "draw back": *hypestellen heauton* is a military term: 'retreat to a safe position.'

2.12: cp. Acts 15.1: "Certain people coming down from Judaea were teaching the brethren 'If you are not circumcised according to the custom from Moses, you cannot be saved.'"

2.13: "hypocrisy": the Greek word *hypokrisis* can mean "pretense, play-acting, insincerity"; Paul here seems to condemn it as moral dishonesty, timorous dissimulation. It gave the impression that only Jewish converts who continued to observe the Mosaic dietary laws were true Christians.

2.15: "I continued": This is not in the Greek, but apparently Paul is still quoting his speech to Peter—at least through verse 16, perhaps to the end of verse 21.

2.15: "Gentiles": who not only did not observe the Law (like Jewish sinners who disobeyed it) but did not even have it.

2.16: "we too": sc. as much as converts from paganism have to do.

2.16: "justified": a quotation from Psalm 143.2: "Before you no living man is just."

2.17: "sinful": namely, living outside the Law.

2.18: By returning to observance of the Law, he would be entangled in transgressions of it, and imply that he had sinned abandoning the Law in the first place.

2.19: The Law led him to belief in Christ, its goal and replacement (cp.3.24) and new 'higher law'.

2.20: "Christ living in me": cp. Christ's teaching that He is the vine, we the branches living only by his life (Jn 15.1-5).

2.20: "I live in faith": Even the natural life of the believer becomes transfused by and elevated by the supernatural life of grace uniting believers with Christ.

2.21: "God's gift": salvation through Christ's redemptive death.

2.21: "meaningless": the legal term *atheto* means "declare invalid" (e.g., a will), "set aside," "treat as null and void"—sc. here by returning to the Law.

3.1: "out of your minds": literally, "mindless" (anoetoi). Paul is angry and disgusted, and he means here much more reproof than merely "senseless, silly, foolish."

3.1: "cast a spell": *ebaskanen* is a term from witchcraft, meaning to cast an evil eye on someone and bewitch into evil. Note the reference immediately to eyes.

3.1: "displayed to view": As if in a poster for all to see. Paul's description of the suffering Savior had been that graphic!

3.3: "in the flesh": Paul means that they had found God and the way to salvation by faith in the Gospel he preached to them; they do not now need to start over by submitting to circumcision and all the obligations of the Mosaic Law.

3.4: "merely in vain": Paul warns that if the Galatians, so blessed by gifts of the Spirit, now fall back into a life of merely bodily and external legalities, their new state will be worse than before they believed. (cp. Heb 6.4-8).

3.5: "wonders": such as charismatic gifts of tongues, prophecy, etc., as described at 1 Cor 12.8-10; 14.5; Acts 2.3-4; 10.45-47, etc.

3.6: This quotation from Gn 15.6 is invoked also at Rom 4.3.

3.7: Paul's opponents have been telling the Galatians that they can become 'sons of Abraham' and share in God's blessings on him and his seed only by accepting circumcision and observance of the Law. Paul insists that his converts have already been justified by faith, without doing the works of the Law, just as Abraham was (who believed before the Law was given to Moses). Therefore believers (and no others) are sons of Abraham in the true sense.

3.8: The quotation is from Gn 12.3; cp. Gn 18.18; Sir 44.21; Acts 3.25.

3.9: This refutes the Judaizers' contention that pagan converts must adopt the Jewish Law in order to benefit from the promises made to Abraham.

3.10: Paul is quoting Dt 27.26.

3.11: This quotation from Habakkuk (2.4) is cited also at Rom 1.17 and Heb 10.38. Paul is adapting to his argument the prophet's original meaning that 'the man faithful to the Law will be saved because of his fidelity.'

3.12: Quoting Lv 18.5; also recalled at Rom 10.5. The Law sanctified by deeds, not faith.

3.13: "becoming a curse": the price which Christ paid to buy us back from damnation was Himself (cp.1.4). He submitted to the curse to keep it from falling on us. cp. 2 Cor 5.21: "For our sakes God made him to be sin who knew no sin, that in him we might become the holiness of God."

3.13: Citing Dt 21.23, which refers to executed criminals hanged in public view.

3.14: "us": Jews as well as Gentiles.

3.15: If even a man's legal agreement is unalterable, much less will God back out of his covenant with Abraham and his descendants.

3.16: "Promises": Paul uses the Greek word for 'election promises' made by a candidate for office. It is likely plural here because it had been made repeatedly (Gn 12.7; 13.15; 17.7-8; Ex 32.13, etc).

3.16: "descendant": though the reference in Gn and Ex passages is clearly to all of Abraham's descendants down the ages, Paul exploits the collective singular "your seed" to make it apply to Christ—as does the singular "offspring" of Eve at Gn 3.15 who will strike at the serpents's head: taken to refer to the Redeemer from Adam's sin.

3.17: "by God": some MSS add "in Christ."

3.18: This refutes the Judaizers' contention that the covenant promises are fulfilled only as a reward for observing the Law.

3.19: The Law both stood as a condemnation of the Chosen People's sins, and specified what sins are. As Paul says at Rom 3.20, "knowledge of sin comes through the Law," and at Rom 7.7-8: "I would not have recognized sin except through the Law—I would not have known what 'coveting' means except that the Law says 'You shall not covet.'...For apart from law, sin is dead" that is, meaningless). At 1 Tm 8-9, Paul admits that "the Law is good, if one uses it in the way that a law is meant to be used—with the understanding that the law is laid down, not for the good person but for the lawless and unruly, the irreligious and the sinful."

3.19: "Angels": Jewish tradition held that the Law was given to Moses by the ministry of angels (cp.Acts 7.38, 53; Heb 2.2).

3.19: "mediator": Moses (Acts 7.38). Paul implies that the Promise was superior, as coming directly from God.

3.20: Unlike the Law, the Promise came from God himself, without any mediator.

3.21: What the Law prescribed was good and holy (cp.Rom 7.12), but it provided men no strength to observe it.

3.22: "subjection to sin": Whoever sins is a slave of sin (Jn 8.34; 2 Pt 2.19; Rom 6.16, 20). and even the material universe is enslaved (Rom 8.20-22).

3.24: "guide": Paul's word is *paidagogos* "a boy's attendant or tutor." This is the term for the family slave trusted to conduct a youth safely to and from school until he reached maturity and independence. The Law, Paul says, was a temporary formative arrangement until Christ took over. Its function was to make people aware of their sinfulness and hence of their need of redemption by Christ.

3.26: "sons": that is, adult sons, no longer under the guidance of the pedagogue.

3.27: "clothed yourselves with Christ": an Old Testament image for taking on a new attitude or character (cp. Jb 29.14; Is 59.17; 2 Chr 6.41); Paul uses it also at Rom 13.14; Eph 4.24; Col 3.10. In the pagan Mystery Religions, one put on a god's raiment to identify with him.

3.28: All the baptized are equal in Christ, one with him, with no racial, social, or sexual distinctions or superiorities.

4.3: These powers seem to be thought of as celestial beings in control of the physical constituents of the universe—earth, air, fire, water. They are contrasted to Christ at Col 2.8, 20.

4.4: "time-limit": literally, "fulness of time," its appointed completion.

4.4: "sent forth": this implies the pre-existence of the Son, though it does not also assert his eternity or his equality with the Father.

4.5: "receive": the Greek *apolabein* implies receiving something due or (as in this case) promised. St. Augustine sees in it our *getting back* the sonship lost by Adam.

4.5: "adopted sons": by being adopted as a son, the slave gained freedom and inheritance rights.

4.6: "our": some MSS have "your" hearts.

4.6: "Spirit of his Son": This implies that the Spirit is a person, sent forth as was the Son (verse 3).

4.7: "by God's doing": some MSS read "through Christ," others "heir of God, through Jesus/Christ."

4.8: The reference is to the pagan gods; or in the case of Jews, the 'elemental powers of the world' mentioned in verse 3.

4.9: "by him": God took the initiative in their conversion, acknowledging them as his own.

4.9: "weak and beggarly": they can do nothing and give nothing, and in fact like beggars must seek sustenance from without.

4.10: The reference is to special obligations felt on such days as the Sabbath or Yom Kippur, months like New Moon, seasons like Passover or Pentecost, and sabbatical years (Lv 25.5), etc. Cp. the similar complaint at Col 2.16.

4.12: "as I am": probably imitation of Paul's independence from the Law (cp. 1 Cor 9.21).

4.13: Because of some unspecified illness, Paul changed his planned route and went to Galatia, and while there seized the opportunity to preach Christ.

4 14: The sickness most likely to cause them disgust would be epileptic fits, making them think Paul was possessed or unstable. But perhaps verse 15 rather implies that it was eye-infection. "Brush aside in disgust": literally, "spit out"; or the reference may be to the superstitious custom of spitting to ward off harm at the sight of a sick person or epileptic.

4.16: Paul is afraid that this letter, with its warning against the Judaizers, will alienate his converts.

4.17: Their "other gospel" (1.6) would exclude Paul's Galatian converts from the true fellowship of Christ, and make them think that the Judaizers are the only true Christians.

4.18: Paul means that others besides himself *could* preach Christ rightly.

4.23: That is, in the normal way, not miraculously as a result of a special divine promise.

4.24: "covenant": namely, the Mosaic Law.

4.25: "Hagar is Sinai": some MSS omit "Hagar" and read "Sinai is…"

4.25: "corresponds to": is in the same category as. Paul's word *systoichei* means "stands in the same line with." One line is Hagar—Sinai covenant—earthly Jerusalem; the other line is Sarah—Abraham covenant—heavenly Jerusalem.

4.25: "slavery": Hagar's offspring was illegitimate and enslaved; so are they who call themselves children of Jerusalem and the Mosaic Law—which was given on Sinai, outside the Promised Land.

4.26: "our mother": some MSS read "mother of all of us."

4.27: The quotation is from Is 54.1.

4.28: "you": some MSS substitute "we."

4.29: Ishmael tried to deprive Isaac of his inheritance (Gn 21.9-10).

4.30: Quoting Gn 21.10. Cp. Jn 8.35.

5.1: "freed us": Christ meant our freedom to be permanent.

5.1: "so": Some MSS put this "so" before "it was" rather than here.

5.4: "divorced yourselves": Paul's word (katergethete) means "empty an association of all meaning," "become estranged."
5.5: "we": that is, true believers, the Church.
5.6: "means anything": is of no avail for our justification before God.
5.6: Or the final phrase can mean "faith energized by (God's) love."
5.7: "running along": in the race toward eternal salvation (cp. 1 Cor 9.24-25; Phil 3.14).
5.8: "him": God, through Paul (as in 1.6). Abandoning Paul's teaching involves defection from God also.
5.10: Though the Galatians are inclined to withdraw their confidence from Paul and give it to his critics, *he* will remain confident of them.
5.11: "advocate circumcision": as his opponents are apparently claiming. Perhaps they cited the case of Timothy, whom Paul circumcised "because of the Jews" (Acts 16.3).
5.11: "the cross a stumbling-block": Paul's preaching of salvation by faith in Christ crucified meant that circumcision and the Mosaic Law were no longer necessary or salvific. This shocked and scandalized many Jews and aroused their opposition to Christianity.
5.12: A sarcastic half-wish that their knife would go beyond mere circumcision. That would make them similar to the pagan priests of Cybele (cp.Phi1 3.2 and the note there).
5.13: "free rein": that is, opportunity, pretext for sensual indulgence. The image is a military one: of a staging-base for an armed attack.
5.13: "one another's service": At verse 6, Paul had said that faith should express itself through love. Here he explains that Christ-like love expresses itself through service—as Christ had taught: "Love your neighbor as yourself" (Lk 10.27; Mt 22.39).
5.14: Quoting Lv 19.18. Christ had said the same (see preceding note).
5.17: "whatever": sc., all your good intentions.
5.21: "envy": (phthonoi): some MSS substitute, or add "murders" (phonoi).
5.23: "no law": cp.3.19: the Law was given because of transgressions, not virtuous deeds.
6.1: "surprised into sin": Paul is thinking of sins of weakness, not of studied defiance of God.
6.2: "burdens": cp.5.13: "put yourselves at one another's service." The verb *bastazo* is the one used of Christ carrying his cross (Jn 19.17).

6.2: "fulfill": some MSS give this as an imperative, others as future ("you will fulfill").

6.4: Self-examination is the cure for self-deception. One should compare what he is now with what he was before, and give credit to God (cp. Rom 6.19-22).

6.5: "load": this word is used of a soldier's pack. If each one corrects his own conduct, he will not burden others with it.

6.6: Paul is always reluctant to speak clearly about monetary contributions.

6.7: "outwits": literally, "mocks, derides, condemns, cheats." God sees through any deception, dishonesty, pretense.

6.10: Cp. Jn 9.4: "Work while it is day; the night is coming when no man can work."

6.11: "script": or possibly "what a long letter." Large letters would make the message more emphatic; or they may hint at Paul's eye-trouble (cp.note on 4.14).

6.12: "flesh": that is, by merely external observance.

6.12: "on account of Christ's cross": sc., for seeking salvation through Christ's redemptive suffering instead of by observance of the Mosaic Law.

6.13: "accept": many MSS read "have accepted."

6.14: "it": or perhaps "whom" (sc. Christ).

6.14: "crucified to the world": by union with Christ's death, Paul has died out of the present world into another one with God. (cp.1.4).

6.17: "brand-marks": Slaves were often branded by a mark (stigma) burned into their flesh to show to whom they belonged; so also many devotees of pagan gods. Paul implies that instead of outdated circumcision, his body bears the scars of his apostolic labors—floggings (Acts 16.22; 2 Cor 11.25), stonings (Acts 14.19), etc. which mark him as belonging to the suffering Christ (cp. Col 1.24)—who will protect his own, so beware!

Cross-References

Page 41

a Gal 1.12; Acts 20.24
b Rom 1.7; Phil 1.2; Phlm 3
c Gal 2.20; 1 Tm 2.6; Ti 2.14; Is 53.6,12
d 1 Jn 5.19
e 2 Cor 11.4

Page 43

a Acts 15.24
b 1 Cor 16.22
c 1 Thes 2.4
d Gal 1.1
e Eph 3.3
f Acts 8.3; 22.4-5; 26.9-11
g Acts 22.3; 26.4

Page 45

a Jer 1.5; Is 49.1; Rom 1.1
b Acts 9.3-6; 22.6-10; 26.13-18
c Gal 2.7
d Mt 13.55; Mk 6.3
e Acts 15.2

Page 47

a Acts 15.1,24; Gal 5.1,13
b Dt 10.17
c Acts 9.15; 22.21; Eph 3.8

Page 49

a Acts 11.2-3
b Rom 3.20, 28; 4.5; 11.6; Phil 3.9. Eph 2.8; Gal 3.11

Page 51

a Rom 7.6
b Jn 13.1; 1 Jn 3.16; Gal 1.4; 1 Tm 2.6; Ti 2.14
c Gal 5.2
d Gn 15.6; Rom 4.3; Jas 2.23

Page 53

a Rom 4.16
b Rom 3.20; Gal 2.16
c Gal 4.5; Rom 8.3
d Heb 9.17
e Ex 12.40

Page 55

a Rom 4.14
b Rom 5.20
c Rom 8.2-4
d Rom 3.11-19; 11.32
e Gal 4.3
f Rom 10.4
g Gal 4.5-7; Jn 1.12; Rom 8.14-15
h Rom 6.3-4; 13.14; Eph 4.24

Page 57

a Rom 10.12; 1 Cor 12.13; Col 3.11
b Rom 4.13; Heb 6.12; Jas 2.5
c Gal 3.23-24; Col 2.20
d Eph 1.10
e Jn 1.14; Rom 1.3
f Gal 3.13
g Rom 8.15-16; Gal 3.26
h Rom 8.17; Gal 3.29

Page 59

a 2 Chr 13.9; Is 37.19; Jer 2.11; 1 Cor 8.4-6; 12
b Col 2.16
c 1 Cor 2.3
d Am 5.10
e Gal 1.7
f 1 Cor 4.14-15; 2 Cor 6.13; 1 Thes 2.7

Page 61

a Gn 16.15
b Gn 21.2
c Gn 17.16; Rom 9.7-9
d Gal 5.1; Rom 8.15
e Heb 12.22; Rv 3.12; 21.2,10
f Rom 9.7-8; Gal 3.29

Page 63

a Gal 3.29
b Jn 8.32,36; Gal 2.4; 5.13
c Acts 15.10
d Gal 2.21

Page 65

a Gal 6.15; 1 Cor 7.19
b Gal 1.6
c 1 Cor 5.6
d 1 Cor 1.23
e 1 Pt 2.16; Rom 6.15
f Lv 19.18; Mt 5.43-45; 7.12; 22.37-40; Mk 12.31; Lk 10.27; Rom 13.9; Jas 2.8
g Gal 5.25; Rom 8.4
h Rom 7.15-25; 1 Pt 2.11
i Rom 8.14
j Rom 6.14; 7.4
k 1 Cor 6.9-10; Eph 5.5; Rv 22.15

Page 67

a Eph 5.9; 1 Cor 13.4-7
b 1 Tm 1.8-9
c Rom 6.6; Col 3.5
d Gal 5.16; Rom 8.4
e Phil 2.3
f Mt 18.15; 2 Tm 2.25; Jas 5.19; Rom 15.1
g 1 Cor 3.18

Page 69

a 1 Cor 11.28; 2 Cor 13.5
b Rom 14.12
c 1 Cor 9.11,14
d Hos 8.7
e Jn 3.6; 6.63; Rom 8.13
f 2 Thes 3.13
g 1 Thes 5.15

h 1 Cor 16.21
i Gal 5.11
j 1 Cor 1.31; 2.2
k Gal 5.6; 1 Cor 7.19
l 2 Cor 5.17
m Ps 125.5; 128.6

Page 71

a 2 Cor 4.10

PART 2

Echoes of Sappho

*In syllable-for-syllable
metrical
correspondence
with the Greek*

ΣΑΠΦΩ

Introduction

Translation into verse has its special problems, but when successful it also has special appeal. Poetry in any language is more than just non-prosaic words and striking insights and expressions. It also involves the music, rhythm, sound-pattern achieved by the choice of words and their collocation and inter-relations. Any change in those qualities, even within the original language, changes the effect of the whole, usually weakening the impact. True poetry is created only by skillful arrangement of the *right* words, those best suited to convey the poet's thought and feeling, in the most effective place and sequence. To alter that is to produce a different entity and to change the subtle contribution of the sound of the words to the heightened poetic effect.

As a result, translation of poetry, whether into verse or prose, is especially challenging. It is essential to keep the precise thought of the original, not to re-write it. In so far as possible, the sound of the original should also be conveyed by the translation, at least its rhythmic structure. The result should be genuinely poetic, like the original, and ideally should end up as a poem of the same quality and pattern as the original—a sort of echo of its musical sound and rhythm as well as of its thought and artistic deployment of language.

In ancient Greek poetry, the dominant factor is the *quantity* of the syllables, arranged in a discernible rhythmic pattern which serves as a kind of musical accompaniment to the thought by its tone and its emotional resonance of the words. In English, the primary factor has traditionally been patterns of *stress* and slack in a fixed metrical design, often with rhyme at recurring intervals. In the best writers, the quantity of syllables is adverted to and artfully used to enhance the appropriateness of the words chosen to transmit the intended effect; but quantity is not normally in English the *basis* of the meter.

To force English words, irrespective of their inherent length of syllables, into the Classical pattern where syllabic quantity is of primary importance is to mis-handle English as if it were Greek or Latin. The result is distortion of poetic structure and betrays a discernible artificiality. The over-all effect is too different from the totality of the original poem.

In the examples here given, I have kept a *syllable-for-syllable correspondence* of metric pattern between translation and original, but on the basis of the metrical principles of each language. Where the Greek has a long syllable, these translations have a stressed syllable—the result being that when read as English normally is read, the same pattern of rhythm is preserved, without forcing the English into imitating the *quantitative* structure of the Greek or displacing its own characteristic stress pattern with imported syllabic quantity which would make the English not sound natural.

This ideal of total metrical correspondence is not commonly attempted. Where it succeeds, the poetic quality of the original is echoed much more faithfully. To maintain such metrical echoing without altering the precise thought of the original or adding to it or omitting something is not easy, and I have failed to attain it with some other passages from Sappho where I tried. But I think it is achieved in the samples here presented, where the translations *sound* like Sappho's originals (apart from the untransferable melody and soft music of her Aeolic Greek), while also faithfully conveying her thought.

Users of this booklet may wish to try their hand at such total correspondence with some other chosen poems in a language other than English. It will call on, and help build up, an extensive command of English sounds and usage. It will also be illuminating to compare the total poetic quality of the same piece if translated into prose.

The Greek texts here presented are based on Diehl's *Anthologia Lyrica* (Leipzig, Teubner, 1938 edition).

ECHOES

Κρῆσσαί νύ ποτ' ὦδ' ἐμμελέως πόδεσσιν
ὤρχηντ' ἀπάλοισ' ἀμφ' ἐρόεντα βῶμον.
πόας τέρεν ἄνθος μάλακον μάτεισαι

Through Crete women once thus to the measure dainty
feet moved in the dance, close by a lovely altar,
soft bloom of the grass tenderly treading under ...

οἶον τὸ γλυκύμαλον ἐρεύθεται ἄκρῳ ἐπ' ὕσδῳ,
ἄκρον ἐπ' ἀκροτάτῳ· λελάθοντο δὲ μαλοδρόπηες,
οὐ μὰν ἐκλελάθοντ', ἀλλ' οὐκ ἐδύναντ' ἐπίκεσθαι.

Like some honey-sweet apple ablush on the bough's
     very summit,
tip of the loftiest limb, by the men overlooked in their
     plucking;
nay, 'twas not overlooked — but none had the reach to
     attain it!

Ϝέσπερε, πάντα φέρεις, ὄσα φαίνολις ἐσκέδασ' Αὔως,
φέρεις ὄιν,
φέρεις αἶγα, φέρεις ἄπυ μάτερι παῖδα.

Evening, restorer of all that the luminous dayspring has
     scattered,
you lead the sheep,
you lead goat, and you lead home the child to his
     mother.

OF SAPPHO

ἦρος ἄγγελος ἱμερόφωνος ἀήδων
Hark! the nightingale, harbinger sweet of the
 Springtide.

γλύκηα μᾶτερ, οὔ τοι δύναμαι κρέκην τὸν ἴστον
πόθῳ δάμεισα παῖδος βραδίναν δι' 'Αφροδίταν.
Beloved mother, see I am unable to ply my distaff,
with love o'erwhelmed of fair youth — and the fault's
 slim Aphrodite!

πλήρης μὲν ἐφαίνετ' ἀ σελάννα·
αἲ δ' ὡς περὶ βῶμον ἐστάθησαν ...
All full up the sky the moon ascended,
and they, as around an altar, banding ...

ἄστερες μὲν ἀμφὶ κάλαν σελάνναν
ἂψ ἀπυκρύπτοισι φάεννον εἶδος,
ὄπποτα πλήθοισα μάλιστα λάμπῃ
 γᾶν ἐπὶ παῖσαν.
Stars about the beautiful moon, retiring,
cloak again their glorious forms' refulgence
when she casts full-orbed o'er the earth her brightest
 silvery splendor.

SAPPHO continued

ἐν δ' ὔδωρ ψῦχρον κελάδει δι' ὔσδων
μαλίνων, βρόδοισι δὲ παῖς ὀ χῶρος
ἐσκίαστ', αἰθυσσομένων δὲ φύλλων
κῶμα καταίρει·

There a cool stream babbles amid the branches
apple-bent, all dark is the ground with myriad
roses, while from quivering leaves a drowsy
   slumber is swooping.

δέδυκε μὲν ἀ σελάννα
καὶ Πληΐαδες, μέσαι δὲ
νύκτες, παρὰ δ' ἔρχετ' ὤρα
ἔγω δὲ μόνα κατεύδω.

Already the moon is vanished;
now Pleiades too; the night is
half-sped, as the hour advances . . .
but I'm all alone to sleep here.

PART 3

The inaugural address
of
JOHN FITZGERALD KENNEDY

*in the language
of Marcus Tullius Cicero*

J.F. KENNEDY
LATINUS

Introduction

JOHN F. KENNEDY'S Inaugural Address when he became the 35th President of the United States in 1961 was widely admired for its spirit and rhetorical style. I encouraged a graduate student in Classics, Jo Ann Sweeney, to put some of it into Latin as an exercise in composition and an interesting project. When the President was assassinated in November 1963, a highly emotional event leading to numerous tributes, I undertook to cast the whole of the Inaugural speech into Latin in the Classical manner, completing the whole text and re-working the part done earlier into a uniform style. I tried to cast the Latin into a level and manner of expression that echo the quality of the original English—which had itself obviously been modelled on Classical oratory. Not pretentiously Ciceronian, the translation seeks to reflect the Latin usage of the leading authors of Rome's Golden Age.

A special challenge was to express in clear and understandable Latin the many strictly modern, even American, words and phrases which the speech naturally uses. Both the elevation and the vigor of the original had to be imitated in the English version. A challenge on many levels!

Class discussion of this material can involve analysis of the meaning and style of the President's language and the merits of various alternative translations of particular words and phrases. Sentence length and structure are also matter for effective transfer of the spirit of the original into the Latin recasting. Such efforts will surely clarify and strengthen the student's grasp of Latin idiom and literary style.

This translation was originally published in leaflet form by Loyola University in Chicago, as a tribute to John Kennedy's memory.

*In Respectful Memory
of the Thirty-Fifth President
of the United States
for His Inspiring Leadership*

Johannis F. Kennedy Oratio Cum Munus Reipublicae Gubernandae Suscepit

Non factionis victoriam celebramus hodie sed libertatis triumphum, quod et finem et principium repraesentat, tamque renovationem significat quam rerum mutationem. Idem namque iusiurandum ego hodie coram vobis et omnipotenti Deo iuravi quod maiores nostri abhinc centum septuaginta quinque paene annis instituerunt.

 O tempora, o mores! Quam diversa sunt hodie omnia! Nunc enim homines mortales potestatem tenemus tum omni hominum egestati tum omni vitae humanae rationi finem ponere. Interim tamen eadem illa in meliorem vitam consilia quae patres nostri propugnabant passim adhuc in diversis terrae partibus periclitantur—persuasionem dico illam qua tenemus hominum iura non de gubernantium benignitate sed de manu Dei oriri.

 Nobis hodie obliviscendum non est nos illorum qui prius huic melioris regiminis consilio studuerunt esse heredes. Hoc e loco et tempore nuntium diffametur amicis nostris aeque et inimicis taedam illam traditam esse novae Americanorum progeniei qui hoc saeculo geniti et bello confirmati et pace tam difficili quam acerba exerciti hereditatem nostram avitam admiremur quique minime parati simus aut videre aut pati illa iura humana solvi quibus promovendis haec nostra gens semper commissa est quibusque defendendis nos hodie domi forisque obligamur.

 Sciant omnes, sive nobis bonum sive malum velint, nos promptos esse ad quodlibet pretium solvendum, quemlibet laborem sustinendum, quamlibet tolerandam molestiam, ut adiuvantibus amicis spretisque inimicis libertati servandae promovendaeque curemus.

The Inaugural Address of John F. Kennedy

We observe today not a victory of party but a celebration of freedom—symbolizing an end as well as a beginning—signifying renewal as well as change. For I have sworn before you and almighty God the same solemn oath our forebears prescribed nearly a century and three-quarters ago.

The world is very different now. For man holds in his mortal hands the power to abolish all forms of human poverty and all forms of human life. And yet the same revolutionary beliefs for which our forebears fought are still at issue around the globe—the belief that the rights of man come not from the generosity of the state but from the hand of God.

We dare not forget today that we are the heirs of that first revolution. Let the word go forth from this time and place, to friend and foe alike, that the torch has been passed to a new generation of Americans—born in this century, tempered by war, disciplined by a hard and bitter peace, proud of our ancient heritage—and unwilling to witness or permit the slow undoing of those human rights to which this nation has always been committed, and to which we are committed today at home and around the world.

Let every nation know, whether it wish us well or ill, that we shall pay any price, bear any burden, meet any hardship, support any friend, or oppose any foe in order to assure the survival and success of liberty.

Hoc aperte promittimus: immo et plura pollicemur.

Sociis nostris antiquis probatisque illis quibuscum morum et religionis principia communicamus nos fore amicos fideles profitemur. Multa simul et communiter faciamus. Parum enim est quod invicem coniuncti facere non possimus. Disiuncti tamen pauca perficiemus—neve audeamus provocationi potenti obviam ire mutuo dissentientes ac divisi.

Nationibus illis novellis quas laeti inter liberas nunc salutamus fidem damus nos toleraturos non esse ut pro vetere dominio colonico excusso aliud subeant multo iam acerbius. Eas semper nobiscum sentire non praevidebimus: semper autem sperabimus eas in libertate sua defendenda fortes fore. Quibus consilium damus ut continuo reminiscantur eos qui temporibus anteactis potentes se esse insipienter censebant quia tigris tergo veherentur postea semper intus fuisse repertos.

Illis gentibus quae per dimidium orbis terrarum in casis vicisque habitantes vincula communis miseriae rumpere contendunt nos pollicemur eos per quantum necesse erit tempus omnibus nostris copiis ut ipsi se iuvent iuvare. Quod faciemus, non quia Communistae id faciant ipsi, neque quia eos ad sententiam nostram ducere velimus, sed quia fas est et iustum. Etenim si nationum societas libera iis multis qui pauperes sunt opitulari nequit, certo neque paucos illos qui divites sunt salvabit.

Civitatibus nostris germanis ad meridiem sitis hoc imprimis pollicemur: fausta nostra dicta in opera bona commutaturos nos esse, societatem cum illis ad earum progressum destinatam ingredientes, ut civibus et civitatibus liberis ad vincula egestatis deponenda subveniamus. Hoc tamen consilium, quod pace non vi progrediatur necesse est ad hominum sperata perficienda, nequaquam permittatur potestatum hostilium praeda fieri. Sciant igitur omnes finitimae nobis civitates nos una cum illis omnem impetum hostilem subversionemque in qualibet republica Americana oppugna-

This much we pledge—and more.

To those old allies whose cultural and spiritual origins we share, we pledge the loyalty of faithful friends. United, there is little we cannot do in a host of cooperative ventures. Divided, there is little we can do—for we dare not meet a powerful challenge at odds and split asunder.

To those new states whom we welcome to the ranks of the free, we pledge our word that one form of colonial control shall not have passed away merely to be replaced by a far more iron tyranny. We shall not always expect to find them supporting our view. But we shall always hope to find them supporting their own freedom—and to remember that, in the past, those who foolishly sought to find power by riding on the tiger's back ended up inside.

To those peoples in the huts and villages of half the globe struggling to break the bonds of mass misery, we pledge our best efforts to help them help themselves, for whatever period is required—not because the Communists may be doing it, not because we seek their votes, but because it is right. If the free society cannot help the many who are poor, it cannot save the few who are rich.

To our sister republics south of the border, we offer a special pledge—to convert our good words into good deeds—in a new alliance for progress—to assist free men and free governments in casting off the chains of poverty. But this peaceful revolution of hope cannot become the prey of hostile powers. Let all our neighbors know that we shall join with them to oppose aggression or subversion anywhere in the Americas. And let every other power know that this hemisphere intends to remain the master of its own house.

turos esse. Omnis quoque natio aliena certior fiat nos omnes in hoc orbis dimidio habitantes statuisse ut ipsi regionum nostrarum domini maneamus.

Nationibus Unitis, universali nempe coetui civitatum quae sui sunt iuris, in quo ultimam nostram spem pacis prudentius locamus his nostris diebus cum belli instrumenta pacis mediis tanto praestent, fidem nostram obligamus promittimusque nos eum fulcire conaturos atque curare ne fiat tribunal conviciis tantum traditum; eius scutum supra nationes novas atque debiles roborabimus; tutelarem eius auctoritatem in plures orbis partes dilatare nitemur.

Illis postremo nationibus quae nobis adversentur non tam promittimus quam consilium proponimus, nempe ut utrimque pacem denuo confirmare incohemus, priusquam vires istae exitiales et atrae quas viri docti resolverunt omnes homines in suicidium sive consulto sive casu citum sepeliant.

Adversariis nostris animum augere, quod invalidi simus, ne audeamus. Tum solum enim, cum arma nostra ultra omne dubium praevalida sint, praeter dubium securi erimus numquam illa arma in usum esse ventura.

Sed neque duo nationum coetus praepotentes possumus de agendi ratione quam nunc sequimur nosmetipsos consolari—cum scilicet utraque ex parte impensis armorum recentium opprimamur et metu iure agitemur mortiferae viris atomicae latius semper grassantis, simul tamen enixe contendamus utrimque ut aequilibrium illud ambiguum instrumentorum terroris, quod solum ab humana gente bellum sane ultimum cohibet, immutemus.

Denuo igitur incipiamus—utrimque memores urbanitatem non significare nos debiles esse, et sinceritatem quam profitemur factis confirmari debere. Numquam sola timoris causa colloquamur; sed neque umquam colloqui timeamus.

Utrimque plus eas quaestiones agitemus in quibus consentimus quam quibus mutuo dividimur.

To that world assembly of sovereign states, the United Nations, our last best hope in an age where the instruments of war have far outpaced the instruments of peace, we renew our pledge of support—to prevent it from becoming merely a forum for invective—to strengthen its shield of the new and the weak—and to enlarge the area in which its writ may run.

Finally, to those nations who would make themselves our adversary, we offer not a pledge but a request: that both sides begin anew the quest for peace, before the dark powers of destruction unleashed by science engulf all humanity in planned or accidental self-destruction.

We dare not tempt them with weakness. For only when our arms are sufficient beyond doubt can we be certain beyond doubt that they will never be employed.

But neither can two great and powerful groups of nations take comfort from our present course—both sides overburdened by the cost of modern weapons, both rightly alarmed by the steady spread of the deadly atom, yet both racing to alter that uncertain balance of terror that stays the hand of mankind's final war.

So let us begin anew—remembering on both sides that civility is not a sign of weakness, and sincerity is always subject to proof. Let us never negotiate out of fear. But let us never fear to negotiate.

Let both sides explore what problems unite us instead of belaboring those problems which divide us.

Utrimque tandem consilia gravia et definita de armis perscrutandis moderandisque construamus, ut summam illam potentiam alias destruendi nationes sub omnium nationum summum imperium reducamus.

Utrimque mirabilia, non terribilia, e scientiis prodere simul nitamur. Coniunctis viribus astra investigemus, regiones desertas in hominum usum redigamus, pestilentias morbosque ubique deleamus, oceani profunda exploremus, artes omnes et commercia pariter provehamus.

Utrimque per terrarum orbem obediamus praeceptis Isaiae prophetae: "Solvite onera gravia...liberate oppressos."

Si denique in suspicionum palude mutui auxilii initium aliquod auspicari possumus, vires coniungamus utrique ad hoc opus instans: progignamus, inquam, non aliud virium bellicarum aequilibrium sed novum ordinem legum in quo qui fortes sunt iusti sint quoque, qui debiles sunt securitate fruantur, et ubique pax tuta servetur.

Quae quidem omnia non subito perficientur—non primis centum diebus nec primis mille neque huius mei magistratus tempore, forsitan ne intra totam quidem aetatem nostram in hoc mundo. Attamen saltem incipiamus!

In manibus vestris, concives mei, potiusquam in meis ultimus exitus nostrae agendi rationis constituetur, sive felix fuerit sive irritus. Ex quo fundata est haec nostra civitas, unumquodque Americanorum saeculum provocatum est ut testimonium det suae in patriam fidelitatis. Ubique per terrarum orbem iuvenum Americanorum qui ad hoc servitium vocati responderunt extant sepulchra.

Nunc iterato tubae clamore nos vocamur—non ut arma feramus, quamvis opus sit armis, nec ut pugnam sustineamus, etsi in pugna constituamur: sed potius vocamur ut certamen feramus diuturnum ac tenebrosum, de anno in annum "in spe gaudentes, in tribulatione patientes"—certamen dico contra communes illos hominum hostes: tyrannidem scilicet, egestatem, morbos, ipsum denique bellum.

Let both sides, for the first time, formulate serious and precise proposals for the inspection and control of arms—and bring the absolute power to destroy other nations under the absolute control of all nations.

Let both sides join to invoke the wonders of science instead of its terrors. Together let us explore the stars, conquer the deserts, eradicate disease, tap the ocean depths, and encourage the arts and commerce.

Let both sides unite to heed in all corners of the earth the command of Isaiah—to "undo the heavy burdens...(and) let the oppressed go free."

And if a beachhead of cooperation can be made in the jungles of suspicion, let both sides join in the next task: creating, not a new balance of power, but a new world of law, where the strong are just and the weak secure and the peace preserved.

All this will not be finished in the first one hundred days. Nor will it be finished in the first one thousand days, nor in the life of this administration, nor even perhaps in our lifetime on this planet. But let us begin.

In your hands, my fellow citizens, more than in mine, will rest the final success or failure of our course. Since this country was founded, each generation of Americans has been summoned to give testimony to its national loyalty. The graves of young Americans who answered the call to service surround the globe.

Now the trumpet summons us again—not as a call to bear arms, though arms we need—not as a call to battle, though embattled we are—but a call to bear the burden of a long twilight struggle, year in and year out "rejoicing in hope, patient in tribulation"—a struggle against the common enemies of man: tyranny, poverty, disease and war itself.

Contra hos hostes nonne foedus grande et universale ferire possemus nos qui in orbis partibus omnibus habitamus, sive in septentrionalibus sive in meridionalibus sive in solis ortu eiusve occasu, quod foedus vivendi rationem fructuosiorem omnibus hominibus praestare possit? Nonne vos ipsos in hunc conatum maximi momenti semperque memorandum nobiscum socios coniungetis?

Per diuturnum huius mundi aevum paucis profecto hominum saeculis datum est libertatem in magno discrimine periclitantem tueri. Ab hoc officio minime resilio, immo libenter id suscipio. Neque credo equidem quemquam e nobis velle de sua natione vel aetate in alienam transire. Ille impetus, illa fides, illud studium cum quibus conatum hunc aggredimur patriam nostram illuminabunt omnesque simul qui ei inserviunt illiusque ignis ardore totus terrarum orbis vere collustrabitur.

Itaque concives mei Americani, ne rogetis quid patria vestra pro vobis facere possit immo quid vos pro patria facere possitis, id rogate.

Concives mecum totius huius mundi, ne rogetis quid nos Americani pro vobis acturi simus, sed potius quid pro hominum libertate coniunctis viribus vos nosque una possimus.

Quod superest sive reipublicae Americanae sive mundi cives sitis, a nobis qui hic regimine fungimur easdem celsas firmitatis et largitionis normas flagitate quas a vobis nos postulamus.

Conscientiam puram praemium nostrum certum et unicum esse scientes, iudicemque ultimum factorum omnium quae egerimus esse Historiam, progrediamur nunc ut gentem hanc nobis amatam ducamus, Deique benedictionem et opem poscamus, conscii tamen hic in terris Dei opera et nostra esse vere debere.

Can we forge against these enemies a grand and global alliance, north and south, east and west, that can assure a more fruitful life for all mankind? Will you join in that historic effort?

In the long history of the world, only a few generations have been granted the role of defending freedom in its hour of maximum danger. I do not shrink from this responsibility—I welcome it. I do not believe that any of us would exchange places with any other people or any other generation. The energy, the faith, and the devotion which we bring to this endeavor will light our country and all who serve it—and the glow from that fire can truly light the world.

And so, my fellow Americans: ask not what your country can do for you—ask what you can do for your country.

My fellow citizens of the world: ask not what America will do for you, but what together we can do for the freedom of man.

Finally, whether you are citizens of America or of the world, ask of us here the same high standards of strength and sacrifice that we ask of you.

With a good conscience our only sure reward, with history the final judge of our deeds, let us go forth to lead the land we love, asking His blessing and His help, but knowing that here on earth God's work must truly be our own.

EASY READERS

38 LATIN STORIES
Designed to Accompany Frederick M. Wheelock's
Latin: An Introductory Course Based on Ancient Authors
Anne H. Groton and James M. May
ISBN 0-86516-171-2   Price: **$10.00**
(Ancilla to Wheelock)

ELEMENTARY LATIN TRANSLATION BOOK
ed. A.E. Hillard and C.G. Botting, with Additions by D.H. Hoffman
A Graded Reader with Review of Inflections
- **Latin Text with readings in Mythology and Roman History**
- **Systematic Review of Inflections • Special Vocabularies**
- **General Vocabulary • Inflections Paradigms**

ISBN 0-86516-055-4   Elementary/Intermediate: 200 pp.   Price **$11.00**

HERODOTUS. The Wars of Greece and Persia (Selections)
ed. W.D. Lowe

Elementary/Intermediate: 150 pp.   ISBN: 0-86516-054-6   Price: **10.00**
• Greek Text • Student Notes • Vocabulary • Illustrations

CORNELIUS NEPOS. Three Lives: Alcibiades, Dion, Atticus
ed. R. Roebuck
ISBN: 0-7135-0037-9   138 pp.   Paper: **$8.00**

This textbook contains introduction, original text, student notes, vocabulary and illustrations. Nepos, being an easy author, will provide your beginners with an early means of escape from synthetic Latin.

VERGIL. Aeneid, Books I and II
ed. Waldo E. Sweet
• **Latin Text** • **Latin Paraphrase** • **Notes from Servius**
ISBN: 0-86516-023-6   Price: **$11.00**

This is a unique textbook: Instead of Student's Notes in English, there is a Paraphrase in easy Latin facing the original, to help the students the "plain meaning" of the author. Instead of a typical Latin-to-English vocabulary, there are selected notes from Servius and others in Latin explaining the words and phrases of the original. The result: *Total immersion in Latin.*

BOLCHAZY-CARDUCCI PUBLISHERS • 44 LAKE STREET • OAK PARK, ILLINOIS 60302 • (312) 386

The following EASY READERS will help you to bring to your students greater pleasure, more effective reinforcement and more success.

CARMINA BURANA

A Textbook by **Judith Lynn Sebesta**
Original Latin Poems • Facing Vocabulary • Essays • Illustrations
English Translation by **Jeffrey M. Duban**
Revised Edition   Hardbound: ISBN 0-86516-049-X   **$20.00**
Paper: ISBN 0-86516-033-3   **$10.00**
SING IT, READ IT, ROCK TO IT

PERSONAE COMICAE

by G.M. Lyne
Eight Short Plays in Latin, plus Vocabulary
Sixth Printing: B-C Reprint of Centaur Books Edition
PERFECT FOR SECOND YEAR LATIN
48 pp.   ISBN: 0-86516-031-7   **$5.00**

Easy Latin, full of basic vocabulary, intended for rapid reading and an enjoyable experience. A lot of *Plautine* Hilarity. Ideal for dramatic reading or class-room staging.

ROME AND HER KINGS

ed. W.D. Lowe and C.E. Freeman
(Extracts from LIVY I)
A Graded Elementary Reader
Latin Text, Notes, and Vocabulary
Price **$9.00**   ISBN: 0-86516-000-7

LATIN READINGS

ed. Gertrude Drake, Ph.D.
ISBN: 0-86516-044-9
112 Pages • 8 x 11 Format
Price **$10.00**   Teacher's Manual **$5.00**

MORE LATIN READINGS

ed. Gertrude Drake, Ph.D.
ISBN: 0-86516-046-5
112 Pages • 8 x 11 Format
Price **$10.00**   Teacher's Manual **$5.00**

LECTIONES PRIMAE

ed. Waldo E. Sweet, Ph.D.
A Graded Reader, Level I
ISBN: 0-86516-186-6
307 pp. Illustrations and Many Photographs
Price **$9.00**   Teacher's Manual **$7.00**

LECTIONES SECUNDAE

ed. Waldo E. Sweet, Ph.D.
A Graded Reader, Level II
ISBN: 0-86516-EBE-C
387 pp. plus Illustrations
Price **$10.00**   Teacher's Manual **$8.00**

CAESAR: INVASION OF BRITAIN

ed. W. Welch and C.G. Duffield
Latin Text, Notes, Vocabulary, Illustrations
Price **$9.00**   ISBN: 0-86516-008-2

If you are not in possession of our catalogue with some 500 books of interest to you or your library, send us your name and address. We'll be happy to mail you our latest catalogue and also our list of 400 Latin and Greek aphorisms on Buttons — a virtual textbook of the wisdom of the ancients — gratis.

BOLCHAZY-CARDUCCI PUBLISHERS • 44 LAKE STREET • OAK PARK, ILLINOIS 60302 • (312) 386-8360

CARMINA BURANA
A TEXTBOOK BY JUDITH LYNN SEBESTA
ORIGINAL LATIN POEMS • FACING VOCABULARY • ESSAYS • ILLUSTRATIONS
ENGLISH TRANSLATION BY JEFFREY M. DUBAN

REVISED EDITION

This Textbook contains the 24 *Carmina Burana* Latin songs arranged by Carl Orff, also facing vocabulary and essays by Judith Sebesta, and an English Translation by Jeffrey M. Duban.

This textbook is recommended for classroom use as a delightful and educational supplement for your daily Latin fare (spend just five minutes a class with this textbook and one of the recordings).

Orff's musical arrangement is easily available on cassettes, LP records, and laser disks. In 1983, Ray Manzarek (formerly of The Doors) came out with a rock arrangement, available on cassettes.

Buy this textbook from us, Orff's or Manzarek's recordings from your records store.

SING IT, READ IT, ROCK TO IT

Then watch Latin come alive — unbelievably more than ever — in your classroom and in the showers.

> My general reaction is one of enthusiasm that this text (*Carmina Burana: Cantiones Profanae*), so ripe for intermediate level use, has received such careful attention (by Sebesta). The introductory material deals with the questions one would expect such material to address and does it with sensitivity both to the poetry and to the needs of the prospective student audience. I would welcome an opportunity to use this in an intermediate level course at my own university.
>
> (Edward V. George, University of Texas)

BOLCHAZY-CARDUCCI PUBLISHERS

A VERGIL CONCORDANCE

compiled by Henrietta Holm Warwick

This keyword-in-context concordance is based on the 1969 Oxford Classical Texts edition, *P. Vergili Maronis Opera*, edited by R.A.B. Mynors. The 83,520 words of the *Eclogues, Georgics,* and *Aeneid* are concorded together. Each word is alphabetically arranged and centered on the page, preceded and followed by approximately a line and a half of context. *Thus various uses of a particular word can be compared easily.* The righthand column gives the location of the word by work, book (or eclogue), and line. Neither capitalization nor punctuation affects the alphabetical sequence.

A *Vergil Concordance* will be useful not only to scholars in classical studies but also to medievalists seeking to identify quotations from Vergil and to high-school faculty teaching the *Aeneid*. Published by University of Minnesota Press. *Available from Bolchazy-Carducci Publishers*

972 pages, 8½×11. $50.00   Now $25.00 + $3.00 postage

Getis... manu lacrimabile bellum/ Hyrcanisue Arabisue parant, seu tendere ad	A	7 604
qua- 'mitus lacrimabilis imo/ auditur tumulo et uox reddita fertur ad auris:/	A	3 39
VERGIL Teachers, 'enis lacrimae et uox excidit ore:/ 'uenisti tandem, tuaque exspectata	A	6 686
You Need This! ...ui,/ sunt lacrimae rerum et mentem mortalia tangunt./ solue metus; feret haec	A	1 462
... immota manet, lacrimae uoluuntur inanes./ tum uero infelix fatis exterrita Dido/	A	4 449
...utatur fauor Euryalum lacrimaeque decorae,/ gratior et pulchro ueniens in corpore uirtus./	A	5 343

BOLCHAZY-CARDUCCI PUBLISHERS • 44 LAKE STREET • OAK PARK, ILLINOIS 60302 • (312) 386-8360

 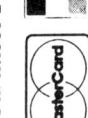

Recommended Easy Latin Readers from Bolchazy-Carducci Publishers

The following EASY READERS will help you to bring to your students greater pleasure, more effective reinforcement and more success.

38 Latin Stories

Designed to Accompany Frederick M. Wheelock's *Latin: An Introductory Course Based on Ancient Authors*

Anne H. Groton and James M. May

ISBN 0-86516-171-2 $10.00

(Ancilla to Wheelock)

These thirty-eight Latin stories are designed specifically for use with Frederick M. Wheelock's **Latin: An Introductory Course Based on Ancient Authors.** The first eighteen ... recount tales from classical mythology; the last twenty are adaptations of passages ... from Caesar, Catullus, Cicero, Horace, Livy, Petronius, Pliny, Quintillian, Sallust, Terence, and Vergil ... We have drawn heavily upon Cicero since he is the author most frequently represented in Wheelock's Loci Antiqui and Immutati, for which our stories, gradually increasing in complexity, are intended to be preparation. For the most part, the vocabulary and the grammatical constructions used in each story are those to which a student would have been introduced by the time he reached a particular chapter in Wheelock; ... To aid students, we have marked all long vowels with macrons and included a glossary at the back of the book...

Elementary Latin Translation Book

ed. A.E. Hillard and C.G. Botting, with additions by D.H. Hoffman

A Graded Reader with Review of Inflections

Latin Text with readings in Mythology and Roman History

- Systematic Review of Inflections
- Special Vocabularies
- General Vocabulary
- Inflections Paradigms

ISBN 0-86516-055-4 $11.00

Nineteenth Reprint, Eighth Edition of Rivingtons, Montague House 1967 edition

This elementary graded reader will provide two desiderata: a systematic review of inflections; readings in mythology and Roman history. (This review of inflections is combined with graded readings.) Examine this book to see why it has been reprinted 13 times.

Catullus: Love and Hate

(Selected Short Poems)

Leo M. Kaiser

ISBN 0-86516-180-1 $7.50

Original Latin Text. Facing Vocabulary. Notes. Famous English Imitations. Carmina 2, 3, 5, 8, 13, 31, 45, 51, 65, 70, 72, 75, 76, 85, 86, 87, 101

This unique edition of Catullus, Rome's greatest lyric poet, is intended for use immediately upon completion of Elementary Latin.

It is distinctive in that it provides 1) a choice, highly readable selection from Catullus' poems; 2) an extensive running vocabulary facing the Latin text; 3) very helpful notes and metrical identifications below the Latin text; 4) below the running vocabularies, selections from English lyric poetry influenced by the particular Catullan piece, a comment by noted scholars on the genius of Catullus.

If you are not in possession of our catalogue with some 500 books of interest to you your library, send us your name and address. We'll be happy to mail you our latest catalogue and also our list of 400 Latin and Greek aphorisms on Butter — a virtual textbook on the wisdom of the ancients — grati

BOLCHAZY-CARDUCCI PUBLISHERS • 44 LAKE STREET • OAK PARK, ILLINOIS 60302 • (312) 386-8